D0854654

700001278026 3

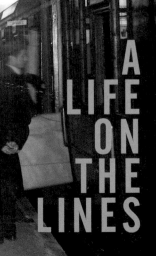

A LIFE ON THE LINES

A RAILWAYMAN'S ALBUM

R. H. N. HARDY

CONWAY

ACKNOWLEDGEMENTS

I am more than grateful to John Lee and Alison Moss at Anova Books who took on this project, and I owe a particular debt to Rupert Wheeler whose idea it was and whose judgement has helped me so much in bringing this book together. I must also thank both Philip Murgatroyd and Ben Maclay (as well as my own family), who have forgotten more than I shall ever know about computers and their little ways. Had it not been for their practical support, I should have got nowhere very fast indeed. And finally my gratitude to Barry Hoper for the excellent printing of my old box camera negatives and the work of the Transport Treasury who have made those images available worldwide and to the descendants of men whose photographs I took at work maybe over 70 years ago.

Text copyright © Richard H N Hardy and Posthouse Publishing Ltd, 2012
Volume copyright © Conway, 2012

First published in Great Britain in 2012 by
Conway, an imprint of Anova Books Ltd
10 Southcombe Street
London W14 0RA
www.anovabooks.com
www.conwaypublishing.com

Distributed in US and Canada by
Sterling Publishing Co. Ltd
387 Park Avenue South
New York, NY 10016-8810

A record of this title is available on request from the British Library.

10 9 8 7 6 5 4 3 2 1

ISBN 9781844861736

Printed and bound by 1010 Printing International Ltd, China

All images are the copyright of The Transport Treasury (www.transporttreasury.co.uk) apart from those listed separately below. The majority of Transport Treasury photographs were taken by the author, but photographs by A E Bennett, R C Riley, R E Vincent, Dr I C Allen and G A Barlow have also been included.
Nick Brodrick 6, Andrew Dow front cover and 19 top left, Peter Hardy 159, David Kindred 83 &85, Robin Russell 142, Trevor Tupper 151, Adrian Vaughan 73 far right, 76, 77 bottom right. Conway Archive 1 & 150.
National Railway Museum / Science & Society Picture Library 19 bottom right, 21 top, 22 all images, 28 all images, 31, 36 top left and bottom left, 39 top and bottom right, 40 left, 41 right, 43 all images, 47, 48 both images, 51, 55 bottom right, 60, 62, 75, 82, 85 right, 86 right, 97 bottom left, 101, 109, 110 left, 113 right, 141 both images, 142 left, 143.

CONTENTS

RICHARD HARDY

ABOVE: I retired as Chairman of the Steam Locomotive Association (SLOA) in 1993 and the committee organised a special train to Dover Marine and back to Victoria. The train was hauled by 70000 'Britannia' masquerading as 'William Shakespeare' 70004. However, the engine that arrived in Dover light engine from Stewarts Lane bore the name John Peck on one side and Richard Hardy on the other. John had been Chief Mechanical Engineer of SLOA for the same six years as me and both of us had been professional railwaymen. The Britannia Society gave me the nameplate which now rests against the fireplace.

FAR LEFT: In the cab of 'Oliver Cromwell' at Norwich.

TOP LEFT AND RIGHT: These are taken with the old box camera about 1957–8 at Stewarts Lane in the cab of a Fairbairn 'Midland' tank. For my children, James and Anthea, it was a bi-annual treat to come down on a Sunday morning to Stewarts Lane shed long after I had moved on to Stratford. They always had the shop officeman, Syd Norman, as their guide, who amused them when they had had their fill of getting on to engines in the shed.

BOTTOM RIGHT: A classic family photograph of Bert Hooker and my son Peter in the cab of 73082 at Waterloo before Bert left for Salisbury. It was every little boy's desire to be an engine driver in those days, although this picture was taken in about 1960 and the interest in steam traction was beginning to wane.

In July 1936 when I was 12, rising 13, I was living in Amersham and my parents gave me a Kodak Box camera just before we went on holiday to Lausanne overlooking Lake Geneva: the idea was that I should take an educational interest in my surroundings, and I did with three scenic efforts, two of the Lausanne trams, and about 20 of the splendid paddle-steamers on Lac Leman – their engines and their shaven-headed engineers were visible for all to see. (I loved every moment of that holiday and in 1949, on our honeymoon, my wife and I stayed at the same hotel and travelled in the same paddle-steamers.) But the day before I left for Switzerland, there was just time to slip down to Amersham station on the Metropolitan and Great Central (Met & GC) and photograph the arrival of the 1606 all stations to Harrow-on-the-Hill and fast to Marylebone.

The engine was a Great Central Director 5506 Butler-Henderson and although my first photograph was quite good with the train slowing up to stop, the second included the driver, who turned out to be Fred France who had fired the engine of the first train to leave Marylebone in 1899. He was then a Gorton (Manchester) fireman but came south to Neasden in 1902 as a driver, retiring in 1937 at the age of 65, no doubt without a railway pension. In time, I developed an understanding of what it meant to be a railwayman, a booking clerk, a signalman, a porter, the ganger and his trackmen, an engine driver or a fireman. On the stationmaster's half-day at Amersham, I was allowed into the signal-box for instruction and I was taken on the footplate to Aylesbury or Rickmansworth, boarding in a cloud of steam to avoid being seen. Arthur Ross, in 1939, a 40-year-old fireman at Neasden, wrote to me answering my questions and Ted Simpson, who retired three months after I started on the railway, wrote to me at school inviting me to travel on the engine of the Night Mail from Marylebone to Aylesbury (if my Mother would allow it). I carried that letter wherever I went, and longed for the usual GC Caprotti but, on the night, it was the newly arrived 'Woolwinder' 2554, an A1 Pacific which suited our driver who was already a Gresley convert!

My parents encouraged my interest in the railways as can be seen from my 'Engine Driver' photograph opposite. In 1929, I was given a copy of *The Railway Magazine* and this monthly gift was of immeasurable value. But when I started as a Premium Apprentice at Doncaster Plant Works in January 1941, I was paid 16 shillings and 2d a week (about 80p) and my digs were 30 shillings so that was the end of my magazine! For a few wonderful days in March 1931, I stayed with the parents of a dear family friend in Mexborough where I visited the engine sheds at Mexborough and Doncaster, Manvers Main Colliery, a glass-blowing factory, and a short trip with the driver of a 'Trackless Tram'. I was meeting much older people whose life revolved around the railway and how I loved to listen to them. Even before the Second World War was declared, trainloads of evacuees came down from Marylebone hauled by a 'Director' nearly always 5505, 'Ypres', probably twice a day. By Christmas 1936, I had saved up over many months and bought *The British Steam Locomotive 1825-1925* by E L Ahrons, a magnificent treatise.

My Mother was widowed in 1938 and she struggled with the school fees, and she was delighted when I left school in 1940 aged 17 and entered the 'Doncaster University of Life', hard but so very rewarding in one's understanding of life and, above all, of one's fellow human beings. I was not an academic and the change from a tough but happy life at boarding school to the rigours of B Shop in wartime was not difficult for I was accepted immediately, not only by the older men but more surprisingly by the mature craft apprentices of 15 (in their second year) who were to start my 'education'. The foreman marched me down the shop and its banks of lathes and put me with a certain Denis Branton (and you will see his photograph on page 41), who was working a turret-lathe. "Hello, kiddo," says Denis, "and what do they call you?" "Richard", I replied, and he laughed: "No, you're Dick." And so I was for the rest of my time on the railway. "You speak a bit queer, Dick, you must come from London." "Not far away," I replied, and Denis said he had never been there: nor had maybe 60 per cent of the work force in the days of only one week's holiday a year in Leger week! My boots were nipping my feet after a week or two of endless standing so, on Denis's advice, I bought a pair of clogs which cost 8 shillings and 6d (42 pence) a pair whereupon I became "Cloggy Dick". Wonderful working footwear, warm, tireless and safe.

Now, the major purpose of this work is to show you some of my photographs taken during the war when films were unobtainable and photography forbidden.

TOP LEFT: This is the second photo I took with my Box Brownie 620 in August 1936 of D11 5506 Butler Henderson at Amersham on the 1606 to Marylebone, all stations Leicester-Harrow-on-the-Hill and fast to Marylebone.

Driver Fred France who retired in 1937 fired on the first train out of Marylebone in 1899 to Driver Ernie Grain. You can see him on the fireman's side of that famous 'aerial' photo where the bigshots are congregated round the engine and Ernie Grain is standing at the regulator in frock coat and pot hat. Fred was driving expresses before the 1914–18 war and was moved from Gorton to Neasden in the early years of the twentieth century.

When Michael Kerry (my oldest friend) and I saved up for our summer trip to Leicester, we had 5506 on the 1655 Marylebone–Manchester and returned with the 1943 ex Leicester, leaving the train at High Wycombe. Fred France was the driver and we went round Rickmansworth very fast. No speedo of course, but those old drivers had marvellous judgement of what was safe.

TOP RIGHT: Taken in 1929 on the front doorstep of his home in Leatherhead, is a certain Richard Hardy probably nearing 6 years of age. I had been invited to a fancy-dress party and my mother had decided that I should go as an engine-driver. But how did one find out how engine drivers dressed at work? My mother went to see the stationmaster who took her along the track to talk to the driver-in-charge of the Drummond 700 class engine that was shunting the yard. He was smartly dressed in the Southern Railway uniform and happy to help my mother who set about taking measurements and noting the style of the overalls.

So there you have me holding an engineman's oil-feeder donated by the driver as well as the sponge-cloth sticking out of my right hand pocket.

BOTTOM: One of my favourite box camera photos on a Sunday morning in July 1939 from Hyrons Lane bridge south of Amersham and where the gradient eases from 1 in 105 after the bridge. Each Sunday in 1939 excursions ran to Sheffield, Nottingham and, I think, to Derby Friargate at 0950, 1000 and 1005 ex Marylebone. They were usually 10 coaches or more and I never saw one hauled by other than a B3 4-cylinder, almost invariably 6166, 6167 and 6168, all Caprotti engines and very good indeed for the job. 'Valour', 6165, also worked one of the trains from time to time. Here, 6168 'Lord Stuart of Wortley' is climbing the last stretch of the bank on the point of blowing off steam and the fireman has put a good poultice in there to last him until he starts to climb up to Dutchlands, the next summit.

My photographs now belong to Barry Hoper's Transport Treasury so that my old negatives, lost for many years, are now in safe hands and available on the Transport Treasury website (www.transporttreasury.co.uk), which is just what I wanted. Over the years Real Photographs and Tim Shuttleworth had done a wonderful job of making prints for my albums but I knew that as my railway photographs, with only a few exceptions, included people standing in front of or on an engine, they might not appeal to all collectors of locomotive photographs. So you will find a selection of excellent enlargements by Barry Hoper that date back to 1940–45 and they are largely of men who went out of their way to befriend me and teach me and make life truly happy for me, as well as of locomotives on which I worked or accompanied the driver and fireman in the cab. As more than one West Riding engineman said: "Dick, one day you are going to be a boss. You come with us and we'll teach you all we know for if you don't know our job inside out, you'll be neither use nor bloody ornament to us or anybody else." I had no footplate pass and those men had nothing to gain from their kindness but my gratitude and the knowledge that they were shaping my life. I was never going to be a Chief Mechanical Engineer nor could I contemplate being a designer nor a Works Manager for I was but a very ordinary engineer. But I was going to build my life in the Locomotive Running Department with all its infinite variety and excitement and its close proximity to those thousands of very independent and able men who actually ran the railway.

And so to my little box camera which did a great job but took a battering and by 1946 was not to be relied on so I bought another for 5 shillings and after my mother died, I found hers, another box which served me well until Dick Riley, an old friend, made me splash out with a Zeiss Nettar at £11 in 1959. During the war, the lady in Bagshaws, the photography shop in St Sepulchre Gate, Doncaster, would let this filthy apparition of a boy in overalls have a 620 film with 8 on a spool in the knowledge that he would reappear every so often and place an order for a few prints, some of which made it down the years into family albums: that lady was marvellous and the negatives, which were lost in one of our moves, were found again when I was moved up to Liverpool in 1968. This meant I was able to have the best enlarged so that in 1969 I could create an album where each picture tells a story and which is now a social history of life 70 years ago where people mostly lived very hard and yet were endlessly friendly towards 'Young Dick'. There will be plenty from that period because men loved to have their photograph taken, as did our lady labourer Phoebe Cliff when I was in the Crimpsall. When I took

LEFT: 4556 was one of the Leeds superheated N1s, the other being 4592. For the record, other superheaters were 4572 at Ardsley; and 4557, 4584, 4598, 4599, 4602 and 4603 at Bradford – splendid engines and very well liked as were the saturated N1s. The N2s, which left in 1941 after the Bramley derailment, were quick in the uptake and strong but would not steam freely without some unauthorised additions across the blastpipe. There were no tears shed when the unwanted and top-heavy N2s went away to be foisted on some other shed. Taken outside Leeds Central station: Driver Ernest Hine, ex GC Barnsley Junction (Penistone), a cheerful, good-hearted man and Fireman Wilf Webster, the elder of the two brothers, very broad of speech and wearing a splendid pair of clogs. Brother Arthur wore clogs until he retired deep in the diesel age.

enginemen, we were usually in a yard or at a station platform, but not often in a shed until I was given a footplate pass in 1944, which I hung on to until, in my first job, in July 1945 at Stratford, I was under the great L P Parker who made you ride on engines wherever you went!

In January 1946, I was a supernumerary foreman at King's Lynn and then acted as Shedmaster at South Lynn for a total of 14 months until 1948 and after a spell in Mr Parker's 'House of Correction' – Motive Power HQ at Liverpool Street – he appointed me firstly as Shedmaster Woodford, then Ipswich and then before I was 29, he engineered my move to Stewarts Lane, Battersea, a year before he retired in 1953. It was his intention to set things up for my return and his successor brought me back to the Stratford District as Assistant DMPS in January 1955. Now I felt that it was not the thing when I was the Guv'nor, either of a depot or later a district, to walk about with a camera and taking pot shots here and there. I thought it was bad for discipline, and I was right, but there were plenty of visiting photographers such as Doctor Ian Allen to whom we gave Dick Elmer, the Stratford Inspector, as a guide. Dick who used to say, "I wonder where Doctor Allen will take me today."

In my collection, I have many pictures of our men either at work or posing for a photograph taken by the likes of Ian or Dick Riley or Roy Vincent, all in the Transport Treasury lists. I might have arranged for the photographs to be taken but I didn't actually take them myself. But that means you have a gap of quite a few years in my own collection which we have managed to bridge and later on add to with Press photographs that found their way into my album.

I have tried to make the point that railwaymen of all sorts are central to the business of running a railway. I had some tough times especially in my earlier days on the Southern at that marvellous depot at Stewarts Lane, but at the end of a year I knew every man in the place whether he was a labourer, a chargehand fitter, a clerk, boilerwasher, stores issuer, engineman. I knew a great deal about his ability to do his job and his personality but not about his home life unless our help was truly needed: but there were still quite a few little dodges I had not rumbled as the present-day survivors are delighted to tell me when we meet at our little gatherings, for it is 60 years since I first went 'Dahn the Lane'. There is one more point that I should make: many of us Eastern and Southern folk never grasped the need for shed plates and their codes nor did we use the extra 3 or 6 ahead of the regional number except with the Bulleid Pacifics and the 'Charleys'. I am sure that you will understand that it would be quite unnatural for me, in this

RIGHT: Leeds Central with a Lanky man on a Midland Compound, 1185 in the background and keeping an eye on us LNER tykes. Driver Herbert Pollard, now a passed fireman and who had fired for Burridge on 4460 on the Pullman jobs before 1937 when the Pacifics, 2553/5 arrived for the Queen of Scots. Herbert had a quiet voice and was known as the 'Whispering Baritone'. Tim Paley and Stan Hodgson both in the second tankie gang, No. 3 Link. Tim is eating an apple and Stan smoking a rare pipe. Stan was the man who started it all for me in the West Riding that night he invited me on to the footplate of 6100, B4 at Wakefield to ride to Doncaster with him and Bob Foster. He had started at the end of December 1922 and was, in 1941, still a 'Young Hand'. But he was an extrovert and asked me, a scruffy boy of 17 looking into the cab at Wakefield Kirkgate, who I was and where I was going and he and Bob put me through my first lesson in preparation and disposal in the early hours in the Garden Sidings before returning to Leeds. And, of course, he was proud of being a Great Northern man if only by two days' service!

sort of book, to adopt what amounts to an unnatural house style. As for shed codes, all I can say is that I was DMPS at Liverpool Street for four years and the Assistant before that and when in recent years, I had to include the Southend code in a piece of writing, I had to apply to David Butcher, meticulous author, friend and one-time fireman at Southend who told me it was 30D, but for the life of me I still don't know the whereabouts of 30B, C, E, F and G although I have a shrewd idea that Stratford was 30A. I have also throughout the book used the accepted abbreviations of railway companies, such as NER for North Eastern Railway, but just in case, we have given a full listing of those companies in the Glossary on page 160, along with some other terms that the reader might not be familiar with.

Here is one short story to finish. In March 1953 our Chief Clerk at Stewarts Lane, Charlie Bayliss, asked me to interview a potential engine cleaner, several years older than the usual school leavers of the day. Charles said that he was something special and so he was. He was very dark skinned, mature and immediately likeable. So Percy Abeydeera from Sri Lanka started on the railway and achieved his aim to become an engine driver in this country. Percy helped to clean the Schools class, 915 for the Queen's journey from Victoria to Tattenham Corner for the Derby. And then in the autumn of 1954, Haile Selassie, Emperor of Abyssinia visited this country and was welcomed by the Queen at Victoria station. The engine was 34088, one of our Bulleids and she looked a picture when she went off to Eastleigh light engine ready for our men to bring the Royal Train up from Gosport next day. Percy had worked wonders on that engine along with his fellow cleaners and when the Emperor returned, I took Percy over to Victoria on 34088 so that he could see the departure and also the young Queen and Sir Winston Churchill.

It has given me great pleasure to keep in touch with Percy and to give him experience of footplate work with Stratford men to Ipswich and wherever he went he was welcomed. He undertakes all manner of handy work for friends and family, he goes to railway gatherings, not long ago with other Stewarts Lane friends, he visited the K&WV Railway and there was old 34092 which he often fired when he was with Driver Cecil Dudley: but he also travels the world and I have just received a card from West Bengal to say that he had been to Darjeeling 'to see and go on the steam engine'. But what better example of the 'Great Brotherhood of Railwaymen' that binds us all together.

LEFT: Here are two ladies standing against 4771 'Green Arrow'. They stand on the ballast, well off the platform at Stratford-on-Avon as do several other would-be passengers and photographers in the days before Health and Safety. My wife Gwenda is on the right with her lifelong friend Pat Carden. They had come to Stratford from High Wycombe behind 4771 to soak up the culture, whereas I had come to work my passage.

The photograph was taken in 1991 in the days when sensible photographers were allowed to take photographs such as these. You can see a couple in action and good luck to them as such a picture could never be taken today.

In the first 24 years of our marriage Gwenda and I moved home seven times, which made life very difficult, but it was the same for most railway officers who had to move for promotion and in fact it increased one's experience immensely. But from 1973 onwards, we never had to move again and Gwenda said when I retired in 1982, "This is where we are going to stay!" And so we made our home in Amersham.

EARLY DAYS
1924–
1940.

01

Here is the beginning of the long, never-ending learning curve of working on the railway and a life worth living. My first journey on the footplate was from Falmer to Brighton (London Road) and the engine was a Stirling F1 with those great 7ft wheels and always with a white feather from those buzzing Ramsbottom safety valves. Once they had been rebuilt with a domed Surtees SECR boiler, they were marvellous old things and back in the 1920s, it was no rare thing to see a couple of them working a relief Boat train to Dover. When I went to Stewarts Lane in 1952, they were well-remembered and known as 'Flying Bedsteads', as they were pretty wild at speed but they were always fast and free steaming. So I travelled on an F1, at 9 years of age and tucked up in the corner in school uniform. The same year, my parents took me on holiday near Instow and the farm was not all that far from the railway so I had a good view of what was going on. Now it so happened that a Mr England was staying at this farm and he held a senior position on the Southern Railway and he immediately arranged for me to travel from Barnstable to Instow on the engine of a passenger train. This time it was an old Brighton E1 class engine rebuilt with an N class pony truck under the enlarged bunker and a larger cab for this sort of passenger work and for banking trains up the heavy grade from St David's Exeter and the Central station, I remember it was 2124 class E1R all rebuilt for the West Country. And then seemingly in no time, maybe seven years, I began my railway career, which I have never regretted for one moment. I have had my bad patches, of course, but I finished on a high note and I was not over-promoted. But the photographs bring back memories, for example that of 3300, a great GN Atlantic with Fireman Percy Hudson and his Driver Alf Cartwright of a wonderful turn of phrase. I got to know them very well and they kept together when Alf moved up into No. 1.

Through the kindness of Ron Smith, the grandson of Driver Sam Smith in the Goods Link in my time, twice a year I go to Leeds and then on to Bramley to the home of Ken Hudson who started at Copley Hill in 1947, more than two years after I left the North. But he followed his father and so did others and when we get together we have everything in common. Ron is the last Copley Hill man at work and he gets a fair amount of steam work with West Coast Trains, often with the Gresley Pacifics and is their Locomotive Inspector. To meet these dear people, all younger than myself, is a joy.

Ken Hudson speaks exactly like his father who helped to educate me. He was with Alf Cartwright about 1942 and we were going to Castleford on a Saturday afternoon with an N1 and four little coaches, a doddle with good coal. The train did not stop at Beeston on a Saturday but did so all the week. The guard came up and did not say anything about not stopping and Alf hadn't checked his book so that we pulled up at an empty platform at Beeston. The guard stepped down from his brake and was about to waive his flag and blow his whistle when an irate little stationmaster appeared and started blazing away at us for stopping when we shouldn't have done. I was on the platform side and had been doing the firing so he spoke to me but as stationmasters were pretty senior people, I asked Alf to speak to him. He shambled across the cab, looked down at the stationmaster, smiled and then drawled: "Well, Mister, it's a long time since we saw you so we thought we would call to see how you were goin' on!", which made the little man even more furious as we were delaying the train. He threatened to report us, so Alf drawled again and with the suspicion of a wink: "Well, it's a pity and it's been grand to see you again but I suppose we had better be on our way." Needless to say, Alf made up the time with so light a load and never heard another word about it. I suppose that the last time I saw Alf was in 1953 when he brought 990 'Henry Oakley' up from Leeds along with Bill Hoole on 251,the first large-boilered GN Atlantic. The remarkable thing was that those two GN engines on such memorable special trains working over the GN main line were manned by GC drivers, Ted Hailstone from Gorton, Bill Hoole from Walton-on-the-Hill and Neasden and thirdly Alf Cartwright from Staveley. Those 'Poggy' men got everywhere, on to the GE as well for such drivers-in-charge as Austen at Sudbury came from Aylesbury GC.

TOP LEFT: North End Gas Works Tunnel at Kings Cross in 1924. A heavy Leeds express, GC 4-cylinder B3 class 6168. The B3 class were powerful and heavy on coal in the wrong hands but there was no option on this gradient. Future Chief Inspector Jenkins, the fireman on this engine, thought the world of her and so did his driver.

TOP RIGHT: The best of the three wonderful Copley Hill Atlantics, 3300, still green in the Garden sidings, August 1941. Percy Hudson and Alf Cartwright were a splendid pair. Alf used to enjoy firing and was only about 54 and was a splendid driver, though Percy used to mutter that he spent more time gossiping than oiling the engine. A very droll humorist who usually wore a celluloid collar which was washed each day under the tap as good as new next day.

BOTTOM LEFT: On the left is the fireman John Albert Walker (Pricker Dick) ex GC from Staveley. He was a comedian and given to using the pricker due to his upbringing at Staveley near a colliery and used to working with heavy freight loads with steam being suddenly required after an hour's standing. The way to get it was to push the fire over with a pricker. Not the Copley Hill way of doing things! The driver is John Smith ('Nookie'), quiet and sound. The engine is 6100, class B4, in the Garden sidings at Doncaster. Albert is 'knobbing' the fire and has the big door open and building up the back end of the grate with good big lumps of Yorkshire hard coal.

BOTTOM RIGHT: Poster produced for the LNER announcing the increase of signalmen's wages. The poster shows a pair of hands manually operating the signals while a train passes by in the distance. The artwork is by Austin Cooper (1890–1964), who was born in Manitoba, Canada, and studied art in Cardiff. Cooper began his career as a commercial artist in Montreal, but returned to London in 1922 where he designed posters for LNER, Indian State Railways and London Transport.

L·N·E·R
Wages of Signalmen
for 1 Year
£1,831,641
Going on All the Time

THE FLYING SCOTSMAN

10 LARGE SIZE 1d.

H·L·OAKLEY·

LUGGAGE LABELS

LEFT: GNR No. 1 Patrick Stirling's masterpiece, built in 1870. Here she is in Cambridge Up Bay in 1938 on a special train of GNR coaches. She is virtually in her original condition minus alterations such as the fitting of the vacuum brake. The tender is not of Stirling design but over the years there have been tenders which could have been made available.

TOP RIGHT: Design for LNER labels by British silhouette artist Harry Lawrence Oakley who made tens of thousands of silhouettes between the 1920s and 1950s. Oakley produced portraits, books, newspaper illustrations, and stationery. He perfected the technique of speedily cutting folded paper with scissors, with no prior drawing, and found a good market for portraits. During his time as a soldier in the First World War he designed posters for the army.

RIGHT: May 1940, B3 6166, Earl Haig, at Amersham. This was the 0815 Marylebone–Leicester all stations, which returned with the corresponding slow due into Marylebone at 1806. The engine then worked the night mail to Leicester in both directions until the Pacifics and V2s were established. Fireman Ted Mahon, and Driver Ted Simpson, the senior driver at Neasden who hailed from Brunswick, Liverpool and came to Neasden in 1898/99 as a fireman. He had been driving since 1911 and firing on the main line for at least five years. He started on the MS&L (CLC) in 1891. He was a dear friend to me and great encouragement in my career: he retired in April 1941, three months after I started at Doncaster.

"THE CORONATION"
ON THE EAST COAST ENTERING SCOTLAND
ITS QUICKER BY RAIL
FULL INFORMATION FROM ANY L N E R OFFICE OR AGENCY

TOP LEFT: A steamraiser lights the fire in the cab of a LMS in 1936, some four hours before the engine leaves the shed.

LEFT: 'The Coronation' on the East Coast Entering Scotland.' Poster produced in 1938 for the LNER promoting rail travel to Scotland, showing the Coronation locomotive travelling at speed along the coast north of Berwick, with the Longstone Lighthouse, Farne Islands Priory, Dunstanborough, Bamburgh and Holy Island Castles shown in the distance. Artwork is by Frank Henry Mason, who was educated at HMS *Conway* and spent time at sea. He painted marine and coastal subjects and was involved in engineering and shipbuilding. He designed railway posters for the NER, GWR and LNER.

ABOVE: This Class V2 2-6-2 steam locomotive 4771 was designed by Sir Nigel Gresley (1876–1941) for the LNER and was built at Doncaster in 1936. It was withdrawn from service in 1962.

ABOVE: At Grantham Loco in 1941. Basil de Longh (on the left) and myself were very young and it must have been September 1941 but it did not stop us posing on old 4040, one of the few J4s left running and really a Newark engine. She was built in 1896 in Ivatt's time by Dubs of Glasgow but has a genuine Stirling curved topped cab with an extension bolted on in later years. She lasted until 1949 and was never reboilered to class J3.

The driver was the hot-tempered Harry Moyer and we were given an 'A' engine (class J6) assisted by 4041. As 4041 was the leading engine, the driver correctly created the brake but for some reason Harry was upset by the Newark man's assumption. Harry went forward and as the Newark driver was not prepared to be got at by some upstart from Doncaster, there was an almighty row. The guard blew until he was purple in the face; station staff shouted and in the end the fireman on 4041 blew the whistle and off we went. To this day I can see the tall Newark driver wearing a unique cap with a bobble on top glaring back at Harry who would periodically shake his fist in retaliation. We got to Grantham and were given a V2 to go forward to Peterborough. This was one of the very few times that I have been on an engine that could not continue its journey to the bitter end.

BELOW AND RIGHT: These photos were taken during the summer of 1939. I was very friendly with an Andover (M&SWJ) driver, Arthur Wilkins, who was exceptionally kind to me as were Mr White and other signalmen at Savernake Low Level. I was at school at Marlborough and our very enlightened housemaster encouraged us to form a cricket team to play against the villages round about.

My favourite fixture was against Burbage whose team contained a fast bowler whose name was K Fear. Mr Fear was, I think, a relief porter/signalman at Savernake and the Burbage captain was Mr Bragg who, I understood, was the local ganger as well as the wicket-keeper. He was the true village cricketer who had one stupendous stroke, came in wearing a cloth cap with one pad and wearing his ordinary trousers held up with braces. No doubt he was a good railwayman too.

So we have 3278 Trefusis, a Duke rather of the old school and I have to say by no means popular. Now there was a Cheltenham–Andover service which left Lansdown at 1335, Marlborough 1521 and the seemingly deserted Savernake High Level at 1531 and here she is hauled by a Bulldog (right), which I think was 3421 leaving the high level en route to Andover. I met Arthur Wilkins again in 1943 when I came down from Doncaster leaving about 0420 and reaching Andover in time for lunch with him and his wife and home in the early hours. And at Stewarts Lane where I also worked, we had Joe Burton who came from Andover and had fired many times for my old friend: It's a small world!

PREVIOUS PAGES LEFT: Before the war, Parkeston shed had a couple of GN Ivatt C12s: 4016 is one of the original 1897 breed leaving Parkeston Quay for Manningtree with some old GER six-wheeled coaches. The engine was not very powerful but could stand a belting. With a full regulator, short cut-off, they tended to bounce up and down at speed!

PREVIOUS PAGES RIGHT: August 1941. New found friends, all ex GC men and posing for a 17-year-old boy and, although they did not know it, for posterity. From left: Fireman Percy Carline, who fired for driver Blanchard and retired shortly afterwards; Jack Burgon, who fired for Polly Hadman and who retired at the same time; and Bob Foster, who had started about 1897, Queen Victoria's Jubilee Year. Percy and Jack had started in 1919 so had 22 years' firing when the photograph was taken. Jack, who was very knowledgeable technically, was killed in 1956 when a defect developed on his engine and he leaned out to either see or listen and hit his head on a bridge near Newark. As for Bob, he gave me a wonderful experience both in driving and firing, and remained a good friend until he was involved in an accident near Doncaster, which ended his career as a driver.

TOP LEFT: A station luggage handler surrounded by Christmas parcels and suitcases in 1936.

LEFT: A LM&S lorry delivering oil and lubricants to a garage in Northampton in 1935. These lorries collected goods to be transported by rail, and delivered goods from depots to their destination. At this time motor vehicles were starting to take over from horse-drawn transport.

ABOVE: M Type container on a lorry at St Pancras goods yard, 1933. These containers were made from steel and lined with wood, with a door at either end. They were ventilated with slats and were used for the transportation of meat. Containers had always been used by the railways. By the 1920s they were being used to transport goods from door to door without the items having to be unpacked.

RIGHT: The C5 Compound Atlantic, 5364 'Lady Farringdon'. I have worked on her on the Cleethorpes–Doncaster line. She was excellent locomotive but long past her best. Leicester had all four in the 1920s and they ran expresses to London which were economical and fast. The Parker D5 on the left is on a Cleethorpes–New Holland service. Take note of the reducing valve on the smokebox.

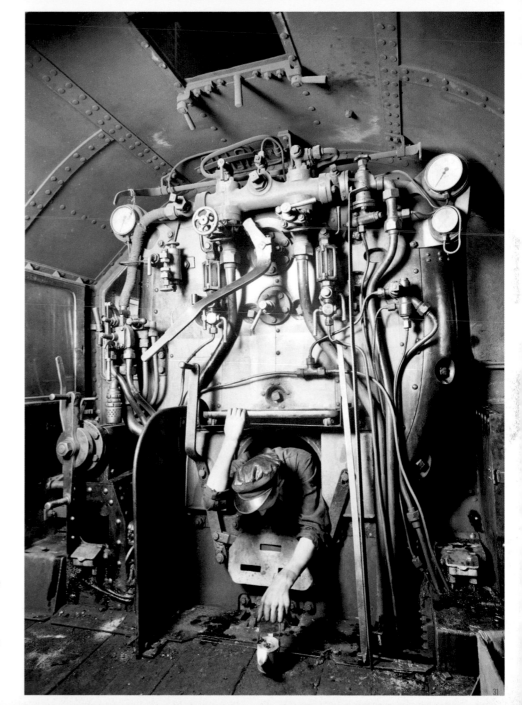

LEFT: 7785 is an F5 'Gobbler', powerful and economical. She is making light work of a load of eight coaches up Bethnal Green bank which was 1 in 70 and will find more climbing later on in the journey. In 1945, the Enfield services were worked by similar F6s and N7s at Epping. The all-important Westinghouse pump is in full view.

RIGHT: A boilermaker after carrying out maintenance work inside a firebox, 1936.

02

WARTIME 1939–1945

DONCASTER WORKS AND RUNNING SHEDS

The Doncaster Works B and D shops were interesting and friendly but a mere prelude to my work in the Crimpsall, a tough but happy 11 months turning out repaired locomotives at a speed unthinkable before the war: but then comes the running sheds, 'Carr Loco' and that was the life for me. It took two years before I reached the Crimpsall repair shop for the first time in 1941. Working in the the machine bay with Harry Oldham was a repetitive but enjoyable job of setting return cranks on wheel sets for engines with Walchaerts valve gear. Harry was a good mate in every way and put up with my inexperience most of the time. Then after a short spell in the Millwrights, fate took me 'down t'Crimmy' again to work on Bill Umpleby's pit in 2 Bay. I was put with Edgar Joe Elvidge with whom I worked for 11 months instead of the allotted six, a great experience as we got on so well together that I asked to forego my five months in 4 Bay on the Pacifics. I had been told by a family friend that I would hear industrial language that I should never try to imitate and I got my fill from Edgar those 11 months. He called me everything, and the more he swore the more I laughed, which suited him fine. As to our work, we were at it flat out as there was a war on and the railways were doing the impossible month after month. Furthermore Edgar had a simple philosophy: he worked for the War Effort, he worked for the LNER and he worked to make as much money as he could, which didn't amount to very much. All of us liked and respected our chargehand, but Edgar used to grumble that 'Beef' Taylor's gang opposite made more money than we did, because Beef was 'good with a pencil', whereas our chargehand was not. Timekeeping was very strict and everybody clocked on next to the Machine Bay office guarded by a Wild West moustachioed gentleman wearing a Stetson who, at two minutes past the hour, would slam the cupboard door with ghoulish pleasure so that you were booked late and lost a quarter. It only happened to me once, and I grabbed my card and nearly lost my fingers instead. I worked with Edgar for nothing and then booked on after a 'quarter'.

Edgar was like many of the plant's craftsmen who had no wish to know the top brass. I doubt if he knew what H N Gresley looked like nor cared: at a pinch, he might recognise the Works Manager, F H Eggleshaw. But he was hot stuff on each Crimpsall foreman's character, although he wanted nothing to do with 'authority'. We had several erectors on our gang, all first class and I was able to get the camera at work now and again when we went to finish off our engine at the Weigh House. Our foreman was a Mr Andrews, who I liked as much as it is possible to do so in such disciplined circumstances, but when I was Divisional Manager in Liverpool about 1971, who should turn up out of the blue but Mr Andrews in retirement, and so we went out together for a splendid lunch at the Adelphi, courtesy of BR. He reminded me of a little incident when I was on the carpet in the office of the Superintendent of the Crimpsall. Shall I ever forget! I wanted to be first out of the gate on my bike at lunchtime and the way to do this was to get into the bike shed and then take the bike to a strategic position out of sight. Unfortunately this had been going on with others for some time and a very senior and terrifying foreman, Mr Whittaker, caught me red handed and gave me one hell of a dressing down. But that was not the end, for during the afternoon I was sent for by Mr Hawkes in his office together with Mr Andrews and Mr Whittaker. I was given a thorough telling-off by Mr Hawkes and told that the matter would be noted on my record, but I felt worse over my foreman's quiet comment: 'Dick, you've let me down badly." George Andrews also told me there was nothing entered on my record card for the simple reason that I didn't have one, except in the Works Manager's office and that was out of the question. But it has lived with me all my life and it makes me think now when I remember how many folk I had to discipline as a shedmaster and the sort of tales that I was told until people realised that I had been through the mill too.

One thing Edgar loathed was to be sent down to the Carr Loco when one of our engines was in minor trouble after being released to traffic. There was no piecework rate attached to such work and Edgar had no room for running shed fitters, who he regarded as a crowd of ignorant bodgers. On the other hand, I was in my element and I knew that come January 1944, I should be transferred to the shed. Edgar could not understand this and told me I must be mad. But on politics, which I never discussed with him or anybody else, Edgar was firmly to the Left, whereas an old friend of his, who patched cylinders with great skill, was very well spoken and never swore as well as being a staunch Conservative. This Mr Day deliberately talked down to Edgar whose temper on politics was within very easy reach, and then he would say: "Now Edgar, there's no call to speak to me in those terms", his preciseness infuriating Edgar even more. Still, they were the best of friends!

This was my education in the 'University of Life', as were my studies for the ONC and HNC in Mechanical Engineering at Doncaster Tech where I showed up poorly against my friends who had left school at 14. John Stephenson and Wally West saw me through Pure Maths and I saw them through English Essay: they both got 1st class passes and I was lucky to get a second: just possible I did not work hard enough.

The running shed life at the Carr was what I really wanted: the comradeship of the artisans and staff, none of whom were on the piecework that drove the Plant men relentlessly onward. Live engines, smoke and steam, excitement, the constant battle with the demands of the timetable, 24 hours a day, seven days a week, breakdowns, derailments, heat and bitter cold, football played in clogs in the lunch hour – or cricket – sometimes extended so that the foreman came after us, rough conditions, no messrooms, no changing rooms, no washing facilities except in a bucket of paraffin, yet this was the life I loved and nothing disillusioned me. Once again, although I was older by now, the men, boys and lady fitter's mates were always friendly. In the Plant, most craftsmen had an apprentice learning his trade whereas at the shed, each fitter had a mate who was not a craftsman but came to know a great deal of the fitter's work and what was needed in an emergency. There were about 12 craft apprentices at the Carr and after seven years of hard training, they had the makings of becoming first class running shed fitters with a very wide knowledge of the faults and weaknesses

TOP: A1 4477 'Gay Crusader' has had a hard war at King's Cross and is ready for a general repair. Soon in the stripping shop, then into 4 Bay Crimpsall, re-assembled with usual skill and speed, given a dab of paint, sent out for her trial, and away down south back into the rough and tumble.

BOTTOM LEFT: A Sunday morning in the summer of 1944 about 1330. We had been on a lifting job that did not require a full gang and for which I would not be paid. From left: our regular guard, Fred Hague, the crane driver, Ernie Newby, George Gant, the van man who, apart from working hard, looked after the cooking, in this case breakfast, probably bully beef, bread and marge and pickles – marvellous. Remember, it was wartime: no eggs, no this and that, but gallons of tea with tinned milk to keep us going; then our foreman, Cyril Palmer, ready for off with his bike clips, Ted Booth, Syd Grindell and Stan Harrison, all long-serving and completely reliable members of the gang.

Stan was a Mexborough man and his brother George was a very kindly staff clerk in the district offices at the north end of the shed. We clocked on at 0300 and went off to Marshalls of Gainsborough to load a sheeted midget submarine on a rail wagon. We were told to keep our mouths shut which we did, for the job was a doddle and everybody bar me was being paid for the privilege. We got back after several delays and deviations, well satisfied. Only the foreman and I went home and the others completed their normal Sunday duties. On the way to work at 0230 I had been stopped by Police Constable 61 at the Gaumont corner for riding without either head or tail light. The moon was bright and, truth to tell, I had set off without them. I was fined 10 shillings. Be it noted that PC 61 was said to be centre-half for Doncaster Rovers by the name of Bycroft.

BOTTOM RIGHT: The Heavy Hammer Gang: Carr Loco brake blockers and adjusters alongside an American 2-8-0 USAA 1720 which had passed through the plant before going overseas in August or September 1944. The photo was taken in the summer at the back end of the shed with Jack Liversedge and Jim Archer. How men have changed in their style of dress, particularly in Jack's case. The old cheap cloth cap was everywhere: usually greasy and comfortable but it provided little protection from knocks and blows to the head. But nobody worried about that sort of thing. Life was dangerous in a running shed but not so bad as all that if you kept a sharp lookout for movements or engines easing up in the shed with you underneath.

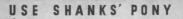

USE SHANKS' PONY

WALK
when you can

AND EASE THE BURDEN WHICH
WAR PUTS ON TRANSPORT

TOP LEFT: A mobile Air Raid Precautions unit formed by LMS with coaches fully equipped for anti-gas training toured the whole of the railway system training employees.

TOP RIGHT: Doncaster Plant Works, March 1943. Left: 'Stan', a Polish aristocrat who later joined the RAF where I heard that he had been killed. He was a most enjoyable character and revelled in the rough and tumble of Yorkshire industrial life. Right: my old mate Edgar Joe Elvidge, who was an erector on Bill Umpleby's pit in the Crimpsall. He was a hard worker and I had to do my whack. I took a few pictures of him but normally there was no time for that sort of thing!

We worked very hard: a small engine would come on our pit stripped down and six days later it was over at the Weigh Bridge having had a general repair. I was Edgar's barrow boy and never happier than when we had to go after rods or piston valves or to the boilermakers or coppersmiths or, better still, to the Carr Loco, which was bad news for Edgar as he regarded shed fitters as beyond the pale. The last time I saw him was in 1963. He had had a serious accident at the Weigh House and was now on a bench job in the Crimpsall where we had a lovely 20 minutes together. Of course, he wanted to know what I had been up to since I left him. As ever, he gave me a rollicking but when we parted there were tears in his eyes.

BOTTOM LEFT: Everyone was encouraged to walk during wartime whenever they could and the government issued posters to that effect.

BOTTOM RIGHT: The Weigh House staff and hangers-on against a new K3 in October 1943. Amongst those on the gangway are Pete Wright and Harold Thomas, apprentices, with Roly Williamson, one day to be Mayor of Doncaster. Standing left-to-right: fitters Paddy Ledger, Fred Gregson, 'Flan', drivers Fred Elmes and Harry Capp, chargehand Arthur Reisbeck, driver Arthur Laver, shunter Dick Ball, our labourer and steam-raiser Dick Jackson and examiner Cyril Wood – not much missed his eagle eye.

Each driver had two weeks on trial trips and one week on 3980, the Crimpsall shunter: the firemen came and went on seniority, all young men by the standards of the day, but the drivers were nominated volunteers and were out of the line of promotion until they wished to return, which was a rarity – a good arrangement as all three men were vastly experienced.

of a large variety of steam locomotives. In the war their work became increasingly difficult especially at a depot with a great deal of freight work such as Mexborough or, indeed, Doncaster.

About the time I started in the running shed in January 1944, the existing mechanical foreman was Charlie Walker who originated from the GC depot of Mexborough, as did many men all over the Eastern Region. But he must have had a hell of a job for he had no assistant and was also the breakdown foreman in charge of the 45-ton crane. A week or two after I joined, a certain Cyril Palmer arrived as Mr Walker's No. 2 and regular breakdown foreman. I was lucky enough to be attached as an extra to the Breakdown Gang after a while and so got to know Cyril quite well, though never did I think that our paths would cross again in later years. He was very brisk and to the point as a foreman and made sure that the work was progressing by regular visits to any gang that seemed to be dragging its feet. Cyril had served his time at Wrexham and probably Gorton but most of his experience as a fitter was at King's Cross and I believe that Doncaster was his first salaried position. He was a natural leader with the Breakdown Gang, whereas I never had the courage when given the opportunity by him to take charge under his wing. I never did master the art of breakdown work but everywhere I went there were men in charge who had it in their blood. At Ipswich there was Stan Stiff who was a fitter's mate, and a wise foreman or shedmaster would agree the moves to be made with Stan and then stand back and leave the job to him. But you did not forget that if anything went wrong, it was you, not Stan, who took the can.

The Breakdown Gang at Doncaster consisted of about 10 men, all normally fitter's mates, all volunteers, who were called away from their work and replaced if possible by a spare mate. Also included in the 10 was a fitter, and we had our own regular guard, Fred Hague, whose normal duties were coal road shunting. We got plenty of variety, re-railing wagons on colliery branches, sorting out a stack of wagons when the points had been moved under the moving train, locomotives derailed, all manner of things.

Here are a couple of interesting jobs. One Sunday in 1944, we booked on at 0300 to go to Marshalls of Gainsborough and load, under strict secrecy, a midget submarine onto a rail vehicle: we were home by lunchtime but there was time for a photograph before our foreman got on his bike and home to lunch (see page 35). The others had a job to do in the shed so they carried on to the end of their normal shift.

At dawn one lovely summer's day we set out for Keighley on a re-railing job outside our normal area. I travelled on the crane with its driver, Ernie Newby, and I had collected the tea and some breakfast for us both from the riding van. I was the only one who knew where we were going once we got into the West Riding and we left the main line at Wortley South and on by Stanningley, Laisterdyke, Queensbury, Cullingworth, Ingrow and thus to Keighley, a very steeply graded line that reduced our old K2 to about 10mph at times. There we found a standard 20-ton brake-van slap across the road some 6oft below the railway line which at that point runs into the passenger station around a very sharp curve. What had transpired was a freight train going towards Bradford the previous evening had stopped to pick up at Cullingworth. The guard unhooked his van leaving it on the main line while he went off to the yard with the engine and two or three wagons. Unfortunately he did not screw his handbrake down tight enough and the van took off down the steep hill gathering speed and, having been wisely diverted by the signalman, went whistling through the goods shed, across the track to Keighley station, through the retaining wall, to come to rest neatly across the street with surprising little damage. Mercifully the street was clear at the time and nobody was injured. Cyril Palmer and his gang and their crane got the brake back onto the track by easy stages. After lunch we were ready to go and I travelled on the engine with Charlie Hook who was used to K2s but he had a young hand with him who got in a tangle and we just kept going at a slow walking speed up the hill. So slow that Ernie Newby got off his crane, picked a nice bunch of wild flowers off the bank and jumped up into the riding van as it slowly struggled by. As for me, I got the blame for the engine running slowly and Cyril Palmer never lost the opportunity over many years to bring up that little story.

I never did unravel Cyril's career because I completely lost touch with him until he suddenly appeared as ADMPS New England, Peterborough and then was promoted DMPS and finally, Motive Power Officer for the GN Line. He did well and it was a tragedy when he died so young.

TOP: LNER workers being served tea in the wagon workshops at Temple Mills in July 1941.

BOTTOM LEFT: Our lady labourer, Phoebe Cliff, stands with some of Bill Umpleby's men beside an old 'W' class D2 4398 and shedded in 'foreign' territory at Botanic Gardens, Hull. We had just turned her off our pit, tarred and feathered, as most of the painting was done while we were working on the engines in the Crimpsall 2 Bay. 4398 would have been on our pit for six maybe seven days, and away into traffic without a trial trip. The Carr Loco would run her in on some tiddlybunk job and off she would go off to Hull. The K2s, K3s and C1 Atlantics took a few days longer and the little engines paid us best on piecework, J3/4, J6, C12, J52, N1 and N2 and such like. Not all the gang is present. From left: Wally Sysman, son of a well-known Doncaster driver; George Sparrow; 'Pat', who had just joined from outside the industry; Edgar; Phoebe, who kept us in order with her sharpish tongue; and George Holmes. It was nearly 70 years ago and it seems like yesterday.

BOTTOM RIGHT: Poster produced for The British Railway system to publicise the war effort. The passenger train on the left is giving way to the one on the right which is loaded with cannons. From June 1940 East Coast shipping was heavily cut back and much of this freight was transferred to rail. On some sections, traffic rose by 500 per cent.

All Clear for the Guns
ON
BRITISH RAILWAYS

ABOVE LEFT: Poster produced for Southern Railways in 1945 announcing the imminent re-decoration of 800 SR stations, which would be undertaken once workers and materials were obtained. The image shows three outstretched hands holding paintbrushes, painting arcs of green and yellow paint. Artwork by L A Webb.

ABOVE: Lincoln Cathedral and 'Uphill' in the distance. We are 'Downhill' at Lincoln Loco where we are lifting in a new turntable for the Outdoor Machinery Dept with the Doncaster Cowans Shildon 45-ton crane. It was a nice job on a warm day in 1944. It was also memorable in that Syd Grindell, Fitter's Mate, dropped the end of a sleeper on the toe of one of my clogs. More through shock rather than pain, it drew the F-word from me at the top of my voice which convulsed the entire gang and foreman Cyril Palmer with laughter in which I soon joined. With clogs, I didn't even lose a toe nail!

Keep 'em moving

EVERY WAGON IS NEEDED
There are only 4 to do the work of 5

WE MUST SPEED
LOADING AND UNLOADING
It's useless making
more goods if we can't move them

A DAY SAVED ON 'TURNROUND'
IS WORTH 100,000 WAGONS

QUICKER 'TURNROUND'
—helps Britain deliver the goods

ABOVE: The engine is an N2 4722. Why we selected it, I would not know, but to three of us, an engine was an engine. From right: John Hyde, Denis Branton, 'Audrey' and myself. When I started at the plant in January 1941, I was sent to learn a turret lathe in B Shop with Denis on days and John on afternoons. By coincidence, the three of us were also in Bill Umpleby's gang in 2 Bay in 1943. I never met anybody less like an 'Audrey', but I suppose it might have been his surname used as a mark of affection. All were craft apprentices serving seven years to become journeymen. Denis finished as one of the chargehands in the New Erecting Shop and John retired as Production Manager at York Works, for many a craft apprentice rose up from the ranks. As for me, I had grown from a skinny nipper at 17 to a fairly muscular boy. Back, arms, chest, stomache muscles and strong hands were developed by hard work and heavy lifting. Try me for a handshake!

ABOVE RIGHT: Poster produced for the Ministry of Transport during the war to remind railway workers that due to a shortage of wagons, they must speed up loading and unloading in order to keep all the wagons moving. Artwork by Folkard-Robert.

LEFT: At the Carr Loco running shed: Flo, Reenie and Dorothy were all lightwork fitter's mates and were all welcome, which says a lot for them in a man's world. They are with Herbert Ealham, an outstanding man and fitter's mate and his regular fitter, Gilbert Holden, a most friendly man. In those days it was unheard of for even the hardest swearing man to do so in front of ladies. On one occasion I was in a smokebox letting drive at some steam pipe nuts with a big hammer while my mate held the long chisel bar (we had to split the nuts). I misfired and hit my mate instead. He let drive at me but with the corner of his eye he saw a girl clerk from the office passing our engine. He jumped down and went after the girl to apologise. When he returned he carried on with me where he had left off!

ABOVE: With men called up, women entered the workforce on an unprecedented scale to replace them. In these images promoting work on the railways, so essential for the war effort, Mrs Molly Temperley does signal maintenance work; a lady train guard begins work at Victoria station in July 1943, and a woman railway worker cleans the tubes of a locomotive at London locomotive depot in about 1941 – one of a series of of drawings and paintings of the St Pancras Locomotive Cleaning and Goods Yard made by Cliff Rowe.

LEFT: About once every three months when work permitted it Edgar said I could go on a trial run if anybody was daft enough to take me. But the trial crews always welcomed a visitor and here we are with the K3 159 which we had turned off our pit the previous day. In the picture is Fireman Roly Williamson and driver Fred Elmes, quiet, calm and experienced. There were three trial drivers: Fred, Harry Capp and Arthur Laver, all volunteers and carefully vetted for knowledge. Two were on trials and the third did the Crimpsall shunting with 3980, the old Stirling J52. The guard appeared from one of the signal boxes on the triangle and we gave him a lift home to Claypole, bike and all!

BOTTOM: Edgar (right) minus the cap that was part of his attire, with two other gentlemen of the Crimpsall. Left is Frank Sutton, storesman. To start the day, I called on Frank for the tallow candles, which we screwed into nuts and were our only source of lighting underneath an engine, whereas at the Carr Loco, the fitters all had acetylene lamps, which had their moments and, if sworn at, would answer with a jet of flame about a foot long. Mr Day (I always called him this) in the centre was a remarkable craftsman who patched cylinders. He was well-spoken and never used bad language and, whereas Edgar was staunch Labour, the old gentleman was as blue a Conservative as ever lived. He and Edgar were good friends and it was a joy to hear them arguing, with Mr Day lecturing from his poop deck the ever more vitriolic Edgar.

RIGHT: In the Crimpsall, you had to shout all the time. Edgar would send me to get the overhead crane but my deep voice would never reach the crane driver up in the roof, so Edgar's piercing whistle would do the trick. Rivetters, welders and boilermakers would work alongside us and the background of noise was beyond belief, but you never gave it a thought for it was part of our life. We boys threw loose asbestos at each other for fun and we never knew we were dealing with dangerous material. The famous 'Asbestos Annie', who put lagging on boilers, was covered with the stuff but I expect she lived to a ripe old age, whereas John Bellwood, three years my junior, died in 1988 of asbestosis. The old K3 is waiting to be stripped for general repair and she looks a rough old thing. From left: Harry Oldham was my fitter in the machine bay; Edgar, my mate, in 2 Bay; Jimmy Jewell, Edgar's friend and boilermaker; Ted Micklethwaite rivetter, who was often on our pit and making a diabolical noise next to us; and a boilermaker whose name I have forgotten. I never cease to marvel that such tough characters were so happy to be photographed for I now have a treasured social history.

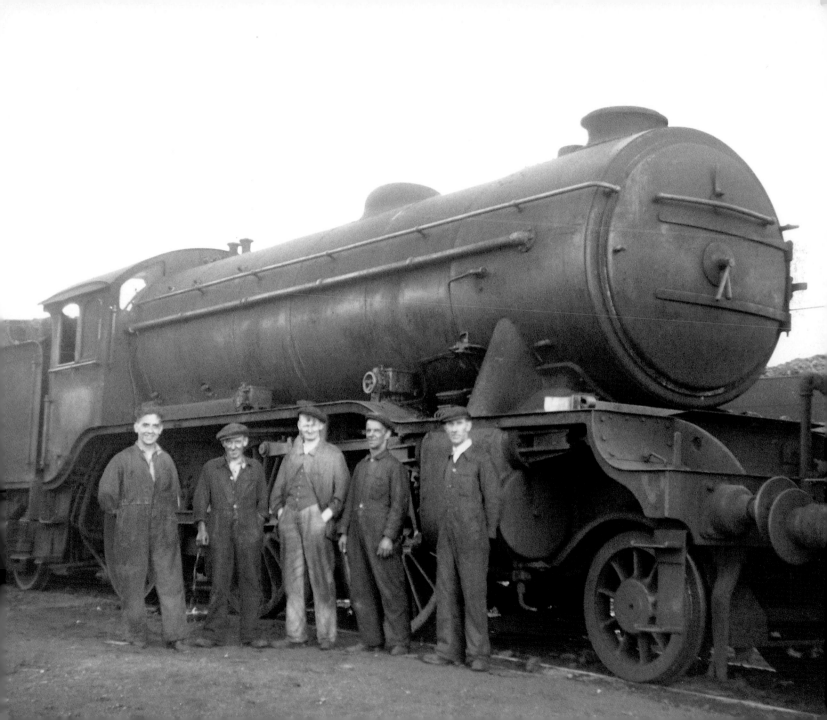

LEFT: The Yankee 2-8-0 1888 had come into Doncaster plant in spring 1943 for some fettling before going to work on the LNER at March. We were not employed on the work but Bill Umpleby and his gang wanted their photo taken against this engine. How different people looked in those days: we came to work on bikes, on foot or on the shiny seated 'Trackless Trams'. Bill, our chargehand, led a happy crew, although his honesty with the pencil when calculating piecework payments used to infuriate Edgar, who was after every penny that could be earned. From left: Wally Sysman on smokeboxes; Bill Umpleby chargehand erector; Phoebe Cliff, our labourer; 'Audrey' another apprentice; Edgar Elvidge, pistons, valves, rods and motion; and Harry Waring, pipework and fittings.

ABOVE: King George VI and Queen Elizabeth at Doncaster works in 1941. The King and Queen visited the works to see the different phases of locomotive building. They met members of staff, from the managers to the workers on the factory floor.

ABOVE LEFT: LNER parcel van, 21 April 1944. These vans collected parcels from stations and took them into offices and warehouses in towns; they also collected parcels to be taken to the station, providing a full door-to-door service. By this time most horse-drawn LNER vehicles had been replaced by motor transport.

ABOVE: The East Coast Main Line and its centres of engineering like York were prime targets for the German air force between 1940 and 1943. In this image, the A4 class 4-6-2 steam locomotive No. 4469 'Sir Ralph Wedgwood' lies damaged in the wreckage of York North locomotive depot, following an air raid on 29 April 1942.

RIGHT: The Mallard, looking the worse for wear and in need of a general overhaul. In fact, my mother was the last to pay the £50 for the 'Duration'. Against the legendary engine, stand some of the premium apprentices. Only three of us stayed with the LNER and BR; it was our life and nothing else would do. From left: Peter Townend, later shedmaster at King's Cross Top Shed where he was the right man at the right time and is the acknowledged expert on Doncaster Pacifics and V2s; Bill Taylor specialised in electric traction and became a senior Electrical Engineer on the LM at Derby; Jack Taylor, who was the son of the C&W engineer and who left the Southern many years ago; Henry Steel who stayed with BR until 1949 and then served the railway in East Africa; Alan Coggan, the son of a GC driver from Keadby who, after transfer to Doncaster, found himself firing on the A1 4481 still with short travel valves and a rough driver who emptied the tender going to London and back. Alan has been all over since leaving the railway and now lives in Switzerland. On the gangway is David Sandiland, and I'm on the right.

ABOVE: In December 1943 the Crimpsall 'Humpy' was a departmental engine but carried its old number, 3980, class J52, which had been built a month before Pat Stirling died in 1895. She was manned in turn by the trial drivers and their mates. The A4, just out of the Crimpsall, is 4466, recently renamed 'Sir Ralph Wedgwood', as the engine that had carried the name, 4469, was damaged beyond repair in an air raid on York in 1942, as shown on page 48. 4466 has just been lit up for the following day's trial run.

RIGHT: VE day celebrations in the Strand, London, 8 May 1945.

WARTIME [03]
1939—1945
FOOTPLATE
STAFF

The camaraderie of the footplate and the skills required were not part of my training but unofficially enginemen went to endless trouble to teach me the art of firing and then driving. During a career in which enginemen played so great a part, this experience was unforgettable.

All three of the Copley Hill GN Atlantics were world beaters and one vile evening early in 1943, Driver Bill Denman had 4433, blowing off light at 155psi, yet he managed to start 14 coaches, packed to the roof with service personnel, a seemingly impossible task. Bill was a quiet, charming, thinking engineman who never got excited, whatever the odds. He had just come from Doncaster in 32 minutes with two stops (remember the load!) and reached Wakefield Westgate a minute early after one of those breath-taking arrivals, the speciality of the Leeds men over the 99 arch viaduct and stopping six coaches past the short down platform.

The right-away was quietly given by the fireman, Jim Edison, Bill opened the regulator and nothing happened. 4433 was a piston valve engine and easy to reverse with the throttle wide open. Four times he did this but she would not move forward. And then the fifth time, she inched away slowly, oh so slowly. Not a word was said but she kept moving quietly forward until, with a glorious bark from the chimney, she was on her way up the heavy grade to Ardsley. Bill had lost several minutes at Westgate so he let rip down the 1 in 100 and the old engine was rocking and rolling faster and faster but perfectly safely. Now Jim Edison had not quite recovered his nerve after a serious derailment at Bramley and when they struck Beeston Junction with a tremendous roll and headed for the over-bridge on the curve short of Beeston station which always looked too tight a fit, he called to his mate: "Steady, Bill, for God's sake, we shall all be killed," and Bill smilingly replied: "That's alright, Jim, don't worry, I'll be with you." The following week, Harry Hornby, the archetypal GN man who had no room for ex GC men, asked Bill if what he had heard about the start at Westgate was true. Bill quietly told him what had happened and Harry shook him by the hand and said, "Well, Bill, I couldn't have done it," a remarkable complement to which Bill rarely referred but which he never forgot. But what a man!

Another time, in 1941, I was going to take an LMS friend of mine into the West Riding from Sheffield Victoria via Penistone and Barnsley so we left Sheffield at 1530 behind another GN Atlantic 3296 from Lincoln. At Penistone we walked the few yards to the engine to thank the driver for a good run. He asked us who we were and where we were going and said,"Well, b—r Barnsley, you're coming with me to Manchester but one at a time". So up got Dick Lawrence and he had a good rock and roll down past Crowden after the Woodhead tunnel. Coming back, Joe Oglesby said (as he was to say more than once over the next four years), "Right, take her up the bank and don't spare my mate." Old 3296 was a slide valve Atlantic so she pulled at my arms when notching up but I found the notch she liked to accelerate gradually up the hill and Joe relieved me before we plunged into the great tunnel. This was the first of many journeys that I made with this wonderful man and my last with his mate, Joe Antcliff was in March 1942 and hereon lies a tale.

In 1999, I gave a talk to the Railway Club which had been advertised in *Rail News* and when I arrived, the Secretary gave me a letter. I opened it and could hardly believe my eyes. It was from J Antcliff to the secretary of the Railway Club.

'Dear Sir.
On reading the Rail News for January I noticed that a certain Mr R Hardy is to give a talk on Railway Management. I myself am a retired Driver now in my 91st year and was stationed at the old Neepsend depot before moving to the new Depot at Darnell during the last War. What I would like to know is your speaker the same Richard Hardy who was an apprentice at Doncaster about the year 1941and was always interested in the practical side of the job and would spend his weekends travelling on engines to gain experience. Two occasions I clearly remember was when I was firing for Driver J Oglesby when Richard came with us to Manchester and back through the old Woodhead tunnel and on another occasion a Saturday night trip to Leicester and back after which I think my mate took him home for a wash and brush up and breakfast before letting Richard go back home to Doncaster. Richard was a very likeable young man and a pleasure to have him around.
Yours Sincerely
J Antcliff
P.S. Hope Richard is well.'

How many old people of 90 and not given to letter writing, would take the trouble to do so after an interval of 57 years since we said goodbye that morning on Victoria station. Unbelievable, but there it was and I rang him on Sunday morning. "Here I am, Joe, it was me!" and I told him that I should be in Sheffield shortly giving a talk to the RCTS who kindly ferried him from his home and back and we met after all those years. There he was, fresh-faced and smiling, far younger than 90 and we met at least twice more and had everything in common. His ambition was to go through the Channel Tunnel and it was all arranged for him to travel on the engine but he was called into hospital for a hip operation so it never came about. So yet again, what a man and the railway was full of such people.

TOP LEFT: With my great mentor Ted Hailstone at Ardsley, summer 1944. We are at Ardsley station in the slow road and we have 4602, superheater, another splendid engine. The day we met, he said, "I've taken a liking to you, young man. If you come with me, I'll make a fireman out of you and then a driver." He was as good as his word, and for many, many thousands of miles I have practised the principles he drilled into me.

He was brought up on the Manchester–Marylebone jobs and, after the First World War, fired for George Bourne on the Sam Fay 428 'City of Liverpool'. Bourne was a disciplinarian and Ted modelled himself on his old driver so that he was not universally popular, but to those who were dedicated to the job, he was a true friend, as he was to his much respected fireman, George Howard, who did as much driving as Ted himself, for he was a splendid fireman and kept very fit. He taught me much about self-discipline, vital to a railwayman, and what he expected of a shedmaster, of management.

TOP RIGHT: A wartime photograph in 1943. Driver Jack Kitching, ex Barnsley and in the Piped Goods Link at Neasden and his ex GN (New England) mate Cecil White at Princes Risborough. I would come down from Doncaster on the Aberdonian leaving at 0420, if on time, and travel with Jack on the 1120 to Woodford via the New Line all stations, even Wotton and Akeman Street and return with the 1505 all stations to Marylebone via the Met. Jack was our 'Inspector' and I drove one way and fired for Cecil the other. Note the blacked-out cab window, the nameplate 'Jutland', and brasses painted over at Gorton Works. Engine 5504, class D11 shedded at Neasden. Jack came south in the early days of the GCR and Cecil was a rare GN man at a GC shed.

BOTTOM LEFT: Bob Foster and Ernest Fearnley with old 6100, class B4, in the bay waiting for Abe Lawrence to bring the empty stock into the Western platform at Doncaster for the 1737 slow to Leeds. By the look of the smokebox door, she has been at Bradford on those London jobs up the 1 in 45 out of Exchange. Shortly after this was taken in 1944, Ernest was passed for driving after 25 years on the footplate.

BOTTOM RIGHT: Staff poster produced for BR to remind staff to label train wagons clearly. The poster illustration shows a railway worker with a lamp, looking at a wagon label. Artwork by Frank Newbould (1887–1951).

5504

HELP the shunter
Use crayon or a
thick black pencil
and BLOCK LETTERS
on wagon labels.
Take care label is
not hidden by sheet

BRITISH RAILWAYS

TOP: York, Lanky yard, with a Jubilee behind in 1945. A Sheffield C1 3273, with Fireman Cyril Golding and Driver Joe Oglesby of Darnall. We had come from Sheffield Victoria with the 1520 flyer to York via Doncaster and Selby. Cyril went in the first coach and as we ran into Rotherham, having come round the curve at a good 50mph with the station in sight, Joe said, "Over here quick and stop her at the platform." This was typical of Joe who always had some unknown challenge to keep you on your toes. That was also the day that I trapped my foot under the fall plate between engine and tender at York. In the yard known as the 'Lanky Loco', there were some sharp curves and the fall plate sprung up, my foot slipped down and I was trapped with the wood of my clogs taking the weight. Joe put the tender handbrake hard on, leaked the vacuum brake off the engine and gave her steam. She went ahead a few inches, out came my clog, the wood a bit squeezed but my foot none the worse – a lesson learned for I was standing between the uprights one arm on the tender, one arm on the engine, rather pleased with myself and not concentrating. The photograph shows the very Spartan working conditions on the GN Atlantics, the boiler fittings can be seen and the driver and fireman were both standing, which was their normal position as the seats were virtually non existent. But the Atlantics were marvellous engines so nobody minded how badly they rocked and rolled.

BOTTOM LEFT: Bradford Exchange early in 1945. A GC N5, 5901, a good strong little engine but with quite big cylinders. The fire had to be in perfect shape and the firing exact and the boiler not too full, otherwise there would be trouble. When I took this photo, I had left the injector at work and when I got back, I had too much water in the boiler and paid the penalty, much to Harold Binder's amusement, for I had neither 'stee-am ner watter' at our first stop, St Dunstans. But, by hard work I made it to Queensbury up the fearful bank and all was well. The group, from left: George Howard, 50 years of age and just passed for driving with his young fireman, Hughie Cansfield. Harold Binder next to George, a GC man from Immingham and a very dear friend. He has the City of Bradford coat of arms in his cap. On the right is his regular mate, Fireman Harry Smith, 48 years of age.

BOTTOM RIGHT: Autumn 1943, Garden sidings, Doncaster, Eng. 231 K3. It's a Sunday afternoon with my mother, a wonderful sport who had lived in Russia before and during the Revolution. She married in 1920 (aged 39) my father, who was 49 and had been a tea planter in Ceylon before the First World War. When he came home, he joined up and spent much of the war in France. Here she is, very much in wartime clothes, with driver Bill Denman and fireman Jim Edison, all three completely at home in each other's company.

ABOVE: In 1944 Copley Hill had more than one Pacific and here is 2552 'Sansovino' behind the Doncaster North box. The hatchet faced fireman, Matt Duck, had left Ernest Hine and was now in the top link, near enough 50 years of age and still firing, but not for long for by 1944 things had begun to move much more quickly especially after the battle for Europe. He was a very good fireman and very strong, although Thernie Marsden was a light driver. I remember when 2552 was a Neasden engine as I was about to join the railway.

RIGHT: Easter 1944 and the B1 8301 'Springbok' is about 16 months out of Darlington Works. I remember seeing her outside the Plant by the old turntable for the inspection of the CME. In March 1943, she went to Gorton and she was by no means rough after 16 months of service. We had a good run to London from Sheffield with three different crews and 11 cars, a very fair load for such a heavy road although the GC B3s often hauled up to 14 on the night trains. Driver Bill Shepley and Fireman Arthur Jepson of Gorton had brought the 0950 from Manchester London Road and inside two minutes they had agreed not only to have their photo taken but Arthur said that he was quite happy to sit on his seat to Nottingham.

LEFT: Two railway workers pose for a photograph beside the tracks on Hest Bank Water troughs between Lancaster and Carnforth.

TOP RIGHT: March 1945 in the 'Lanky Loco' on the up side at York station. Driver Joe Oglesby of Darnall was a lovely man and the sort of mate that firemen dreamed of, and so did I. We became very great friends and I fired for him to Manchester, Leicester, York, Cleethorpes and once to Liverpool. We had worked the 1520 SO Sheffield–York via Rotherham (GC) Mexborough, Doncaster and Selby. Joe always had a surprise up his sleeve. I fired for him on this journey with his mate Cyril Golding in the train. We stopped at Selby after a real dash across the flat from Doncaster. Joe asked, "What have you got in there?" (meaning the firebox). "Enough for York when it's levelled with the poker." "Right, take her to Challoners Whin", and over the other side I went for the final stretch to the outskirts of York. Our engine is 4452, a Sheffield Atlantic, the first piston valve superheated C1 built at Doncaster in 1910.

BOTTOM RIGHT: A remarkable pair. The fireman, Percy Thorpe, is on the gangway with Benny Faux of Ardsley, as always doing the driving on a C14 en route to Ranskill Munitions Factory at Doncaster, taking water. Benny was an amazing character. He was, to some extent, a daredevil who enjoyed himself at work but never talked about it off the job. He knew exactly what he was doing but if he could shock his comrades, he would do so. He took me under his wing and taught me some of the dodges that management was not supposed to know. I was nearly always the driver when I went with him and he would leave it all to Percy and me, taking no apparent interest in what we were doing. But when he had a younger fireman, he was every button on duty and did his own job. My great mentor, Ted Hailstone, would never have dreamt of letting me see the seamy side of the job and used to grumble "I can't think what you see in that Faux!",

LMS

THE DAY BEGINS

LEFT: Poster produced for the LMS in 1946 showing the locomotive 'City of Hereford' undergoing early morning maintenance on a turntable surrounded by various LMS engines in the Willesden depot, London. Artwork by Terence Cuneo, son of the artists Cyrus and Nell Cuneo. He studied at the Chelsea and Slade Art Schools and in addition to a long career designing railway posters, he painted portraits and ceremonial and military subjects.

RIGHT: We had reached Aylesbury after a perfect journey with the B1 8301 'Springbok' and there was just time to take this photo of my friend from home, Donald Douglas, and next to him, Driver Jack Proctor, by then the senior driver at the Neasden, and an old friend from my boyhood days, together with Fireman Charlie Simpson, who lost his life at Barby in 1955.

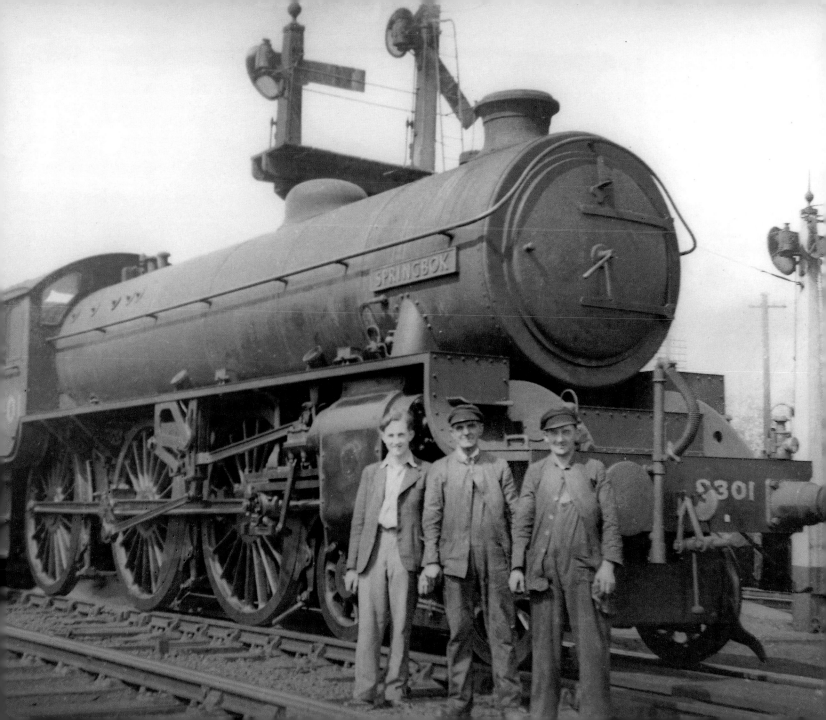

BELOW: 4406, a piston valve Atlantic class C1 was turned out of Doncaster Works just before Christmas 1943, a fortnight before I left the Plant for the Carr Loco. It is in steam and will go on its trial trip next day when Dick Jackson, Weigh House labourer, has coaled it. One of the three trial drivers, Harry Capp, Fred Elmes or Arthur Laver would be in charge of the engine. The piston valve engines had a round piston gland, most of them had dummy tailrod guides and most, but not all, had smokebox saddles. All slide valve engines had oval piston glands and the spindle glands tended to blow, in cold weather, up the boiler side when starting. No wonder with a 32 element superheater these engines were 'world beaters'. The livery is shown to perfection. From 1941, if not before, all engines were turned out of Doncaster and other works in unlined black, and the painting was done not in the paint shop but on the engine as it was being assembled by us!

LEFT: A J52, 4250, on the downside carriage pilot at Doncaster station in the Western bay platform, 1945. On the left is driver Abe Lawrence, always on the late turn, and he used to view my activities with the Leeds men with a jaundiced eye until we got to know each other and he became kindness itself. Shunting was carried out carefully, no histrionics and without hurry, but always to time. Normally, the fireman (a young hand) was never allowed to drive but today he has Charlie Carter, a passed fireman so Abe spent the day on the other side, a pleasant change. The old J52s were everywhere on the GN from London to Doncaster: not many in the West Riding where the pilot and freight work was carried out by the 'Tango tanks', class J50, which were more powerful and so could cope with the fearful gradients in the West Riding.

BELOW: A Doncaster C1 which started life as 1421, a 4-cylinder compound built in 1907 but converted to a piston valve 2-cylinder superheated Atlantic in 1920. As a compound her fireman for some time was George Wilson in the top link along with his brother Fred in my time at Doncaster. We are at Botanic Gardens on a Sunday afternoon with Fireman Arthur Gell and the fiery Harry Moyer who had a brother at Grimsby, a GC man and some years older than Harry who was in the Atlantic link. Harry got on well with Arthur, who was in a lower link and who had changed over with Harry's regular mate with whom he did not get on too well for Harry was not by any means sunshine and light with his regular mates if they did not measure up. He was a very good engineman and a perfectionist and nothing wrong with that.

LEFT: Probably the only photograph taken at the Thorp Arch factory, which was an enormous wartime munitions works. It was taken in June 1945, in the sidings where the trains were stabled between arrival and departure. We brought the incoming shift on duty and went round the factory railway with its four stations. We stabled the train, turned on the angle, and coupled up once more to our train to go tender first round the factory picking up the shift going home; run round once more and right away home. On Saturday and Sunday nights, we had the railway to ourselves and could get home as quick as it was safe to do.

We stopped at Castleford, Normanton and Kirkgate to set down before roaring up to Westgate in the early hours. But this is a Sunday afternoon and we have the best of the very good bunch of B4s, 6101, a real clipper. On the left, we have a factory policeman. While we were at war, the factory police were everywhere watching to see we did not move away from our engine. Then we have our guard, with a trilby hat worn for the occasion. He was a lovely man, endlessly helpful, who was normally a Westgate passenger shunter, and he earned his living alright. Then, in the centre, is Alistair Kerr who was Deputy Land Agent at the County Hall in Wakefield, a vastly knowledgeable student of railway affairs who knew Benny Faux well and later married his daughter, Elsie. Leaning on the buffer with his cap over his nose is Benny himself, then his fireman for the day, Fred Wilson, and finally the Thorp Arch Yard Foreman, Mr Cattermole, whose son was a Darlington premium apprentice some years younger than me.

RIGHT: The old Bradford C12, 4524, spent much of her time working between Bradford, Halifax and Keithley. Driver George Hutchinson was a pleasant man but camera shy – the only West Riding engineman I met who did not want his photo taken. We have taken on water at Keithley in the GN platforms and the fireman, Stan Pilsworth, poses with pleasure. 4524 clawed her way very well up the bank to Ingrow, which we believed to be a much heavier road than the Midland Worth Valley branch that had a poor old Midland tank engine, not given, in our opinion, to heavy work. We thought nothing of the Midland and the Lanky was just bearable!

TOP LEFT: A Sunday, 1400, early 1944. Garden sidings, Doncaster: Fred Holdsworth and myself, now growing out of my overalls. K3 231 is waiting to go up to the station to work on down expresss from King's Cross, which was four hours away with those huge trains during the war. Fred had been a long time in the goods Link at Copley Hill but had moved up into No. 2 Tanky Gang and his mate who took the photograph was my friend Stan Hodgson who had done so much back in 1941 to introduce me to the West Riding. Stan actually came to my retirement party in 1982: what a gathering that was and how Gwenda and the family enjoyed themselves. Fred was an old GC man from Wakefield shed when it closed in 1924 and he loved his clogs. He was a very good engineman which pleased Stan who expected Fred, as a Poggy man (nickname for men who worked on the Great Central), to be heavy handed. As for me, I had to scrounge overalls and cap, and I was never short, but either I had grown or they had shrunk!

BOTTOM LEFT: A Sunday afternoon in 1944 behind the North signalbox. A Doncaster V2 in place of a K3, with Johnny Jeffs (right) and Syd Watson. Johnny was Chairman of the LDC, I think: a very good engineman and very kind to me but hot-tempered so I was told, but I had no experience of LDCs in those days. I was to find that the fiery man was often a 100 per center and both Johnny and his colleague, Ernest Clarke, were straight and to the point. Syd was also splendid value. In 2010 Barry Hoper had an email from a lady in Brisbane who was tracing her family tree. Some of her family lived in Leeds by the name of Jeffs and I had taken a photograph of Driver Johnny Jeffs in 1944–5 which is on the Transport Treasury website. We sent her the picture and some others and in the end I was linked up to Tom Jeffs (Johnny's son) and his son John, and was able to link them up with Barbara Tuck in Australia. When I first traced Tom on the phone we spent 45 minutes talking about Copley Hill men, which gave us both the greatest pleasure. He was going to be 90 in four days time and Barry had some of the Copley Hill photos printed for him and to arrive on his birthday. What could be better?

LEFT: The late summer of 1942 not long before Jack Burgon went up to pass for driving early in 1943. A splendid portrait of both men: Jack Burgon, the great enthusiast despite his 23 years' firing and Arthur Moss with his arthritis so bad that it was a struggle to get up and down from the cab, and yet he did his work without complaint. No doubt, Jack did the oiling and examination for him. Arthur was inclined to be heavy with an engine and did not run downhill very fast but they got on remarkably well. Arthur has a nice pair of clogs. The engine was one of the Doncaster new V2s in the 365 series, built at Darlington in 1942. Why Copley Hill had her on what was normally a K3 turn, I cannot remember. The set on the right is old NER stock, probably a Hull set. Botanic men came into the Garden sidings about 2030 and stood alongside us. The V2 would work the 2201 ex London back to Leeds on double summer time.

EAST ANGLIA AND WOODFORD HALSE

1946–1952.

04

King's Lynn, South Lynn, Woodford Halse and Ipswich. Supernumerary Foreman at Lynn Loco, Acting Shedmaster at South Lynn, Shedmaster at Woodford and Ipswich packed into six years, 1946–52, but what experience for a young man. The two Lynns glared at each other across the town for they were different in every way and yet part of the Cambridge District along with the likes of March, Bury and Cambridge itself. One was ex Great Eastern, the other was 'The Joint', Midland and Great Northern through and through. At South Lynn, some enginemen still wore the Midland shiny top caps and LMS overalls but they had learned to respect the Great Central D9s, the Great Northern 'W's' and the Great Eastern 'Clauds' which replaced their worn-out but much-loved Midland designs.

The men were different. White bristling or sweeping moustaches abounded on the M&GN but I cannot recall one at Lynn Loco. The fitters such as Ernie Eke and the Chargehand Boilermaker George Fuller Pilch were trained in their art at Melton Constable Works, a centre of knowledge deep in the Norfolk countryside. As for the two shedmasters, Ted Shaw ruled supreme at Lynn Loco, as tough as they come but willing to teach a young man if he could take the pressure, which I could. At South Lynn, where I relieved the incumbent, Peter Glenister, as shedmaster for a total of 14 months over two years, was, an ex LNER pupil, charming, laid back but liked and respected. But it was the rough Ted Shaw who showed me how to manipulate the mileage of some old crock without it turning a wheel to get it into Stratford Works for repair, a secret ruse I used sparingly but to advantage in the years ahead.

Just before I left South Lynn for Motive Power HQ under the great L P Parker, the B12s started to come to the M&GN, but at Yarmouth Beach shed for a start. The Joint men worshipped them but one unforgettable day, 1530 arrived on a tight turn-round job with a firebox fusible plug leaking slightly. There was no suitable replacement which meant a serious delay to the return working. The driver assured me he had not been short of water in the boiler but the rules governing such a failure were strict. However, when I told George Pilch, he asked me to have the fire pushed forward and the boiler well filled to knock the pressure back and said what he was going to do was 'not for your eyes, off you go and have your lunch". But I stayed to see him wrap himself in damp sacking, ease himself into the firebox, do something to the fusible and climb out of that hellish firebox. "OK for Yarmouth," was all he said and a quiet word with the driver to keep his mouth shut. George was a master of his craft and never regarded this as dangerous: he was more concerned that there should be no delay to the train – truly a railwayman and a craftsman.

So, in September 1949, L P Parker directed me to take charge at Woodford in Northants but only 10 miles from Banbury. We had 50 engines, B17 and V2s for the passenger and fitted freight work, WD Austerities for the heavy and fast freight jobs to Neasden with some excellent craftsmen to maintain the fleet, but terrible water so that the boilers and fireboxes needed constant attention. We were desperately short of firemen and cleaners, because nobody fancied railway work but we managed somehow and with great pleasure. We had about 250 men, mostly footplate staff and we had a few passenger jobs to London and Nottingham and, of course, the cross-country services from Banbury to the North. But it was mostly freight for which we longed to have O1s and some old RODs but we lumbered with WD Austerities. But we also had eight 'Poms-Poms' class J11 and they would bring 80 empties up from Quainton Road with ease and stand in on a passenger train to London at a pinch.

Woodford was full of characters and no more so than 'Pom' French, Running Foreman, of the stentorian voice and utter determination to run the railway. He loved the job and when he retired he became a passenger guard. He would chivvy up any laggard passengers and as for enginemen, all of whom he knew well, he would say reproachfully that "Time is time" if only half a minute had been lost. Dear Pom – we had so much in common. There are only two Woodford photographs herein and taken at a later date which will speak for themselves.

Gwenda and I were truly happy in our little cottage in the village of Eydon near Woodford and then without warning, I was whisked off to East Anglia by the all-powerful L P Parker. My boss, equally surprised, had a word with L P Parker who said that "If Hardy doesn't go to Ipswich, he won't go anywhere for a very long time." Much to my amazement, I was appointed Shedmaster four days later. Ipswich was said to be a handful and, in some ways, it was but the Suffolkers were very good railwaymen. The original depot dated back to the 1840s but the main part came a little later. We had 91 engines, coaled by hand by coalmen standing on the top of coal wagons or shovelling out of the side door on a trestle. Disposal pits were virtually non existent but the work got done quickly and with ingenuity. Three chargehand fitters did all daily examinations and our engines were in excellent order despite the lack of pits and bad working conditions. Whatever needed doing was done well by the finest group of artisans I ever encountered and led by Jack Percy and Charlie Winney, Leading Fitter and Boilermaker respectively, two men who had forgotten more than many of us would ever know. Engines? We had all sorts, young and old, but for passenger work we had a B1 and a B12 link, each engine being shared by two sets of men which they treated as their own. How do you determine 'pride in the job'? Certainly you cannot put a price on it but it was my duty to encourage it with all my strength.

TOP RIGHT: Ron Alder and Hector Boot at Marylebone last week of the GC London Extension. Ron and I were at Woodford at the same time. He was then a Fireman and also Chairman of the ASLEF Branch. He was said to be a difficult customer but in fact we had it right from the start, a splendid relationship. In time Ron had to make his mind up whether to go full time with his union or to seek promotion into the management grades. He chose the latter and he chose well because without changing his methods he became a first class manager. The engine is a decrepit Black Five but we coaxed it to Woodford. To sum it up, we had a wonderful time with old colleagues and made our way home on the last train up which I had the pleasure of driving with a good Black Five, Driver George Cave.

BOTTOM RIGHT: Woodford station waiting for the last one up, a few days before closure in 1966. I'm in the centre with the Secretary of the Local Department Committee, Driver George Wootton, and the Chairman, Driver Charlie Sanders, both of whom had retired. What a wonderful pair. Good fighters for what was right and as straight as a table top, therefore we worked in perfect accord.

FAR RIGHT: A rare photograph of a 'Four wheeled Tram' in Lynn Loco for repairs beyond the capability of the little shed at Wisbech. This tram was built in 1897 and preceded the larger J70s which were far more powerful. For all that, my one journey down the 'tram', as it was called, was with this engine, 7133 and Driver Potter who came from Gorton for a regular driver's job. But 7133 was also ideally designed for photography. Here we have left-to-right: 'Podmore', who was a mystery man for he worked both as a boilerwasher and a shed labourer and I think a fitter's mate. He was Podmore to everybody, no more no less. Then there is Ted Peck, one of the many railway Pecks at the two sheds, who was a boilerwasher, and Josh Johnson. He and Ted have done the washing out and Podmore has tagged along. There were several men at the two Lynns born in 1899–1900 and named after Boer War generals: Baden Wright was a boilerwasher at King's Lynn, and a very grandly named driver at South Lynn was Redvers Buller Richardson. Despite his name, there was nothing grand about Buller Richardson, as well I know!

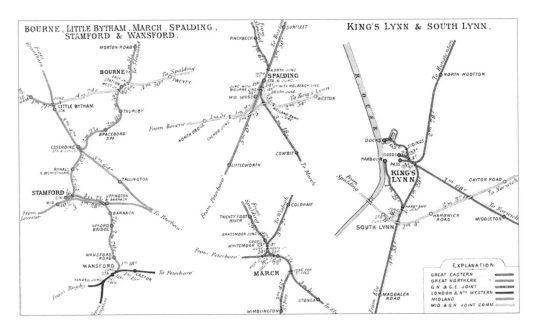

BOURNE, LITTLE BYTHAM, MARCH, SPALDING, STAMFORD & WANSFORD.

KING'S LYNN & SOUTH LYNN.

EXPLANATION

GREAT EASTERN
GREAT NORTHERN
G.N. & G.E. JOINT
LONDON & Nᵗʰ WESTERN
MIDLAND
MID. & G.N. JOINT COMM

LEFT: The purple lines are the the old GER and the yellow lines are the M&GN Joint. In 1946–8, the lines were as shown here in 1915, although Hardwick Road station had gone by then. The Docks and Harbour branches in practice seemed a complicated maze, but not so in the map. Shunting engines were hard at work during weekdays. The three main lines out to Hunstanton, Dereham and Ely are noted and well-used in the summer especially. The M&GN was closed in 1959, well before the Beeching era and the General Manager of the Eastern Region took the decision to close, as was his right. The bridge over the Ouse was known as West Lynn Bridge and the yards were a hive of activity on weekdays. As for the summer in peacetime with the railway largely single line and heavily graded, miracles of haulage by out-dated M&GN locomotives were performed as a matter of routine.

RIGHT: LNER poster advertising weekly holiday season tickets, eastern counties (Area No. 5).

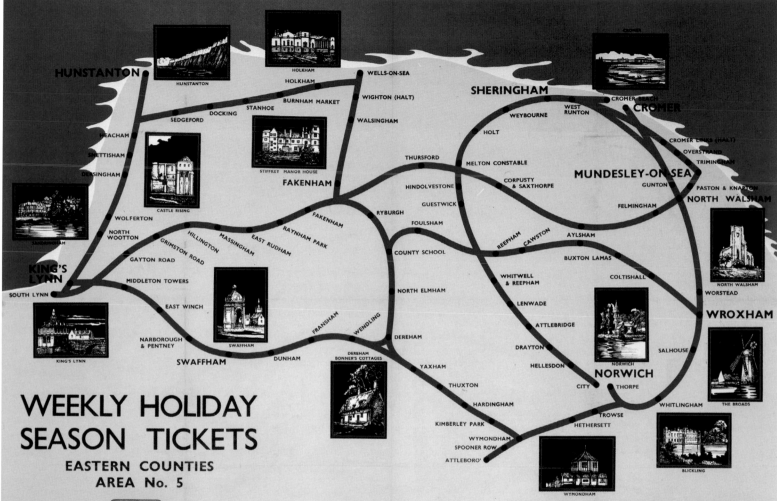

WEEKLY HOLIDAY SEASON TICKETS

EASTERN COUNTIES AREA No. 5

10/6 THIRD CLASS   **15/9** FIRST CLASS

TRAVEL AS OFTEN AS YOU LIKE IN THIS AREA FOR A WEEK

There are 29 districts in England and 20 in Scotland for which similar tickets are issued

FULL DETAILS CAN BE OBTAINED AT L·N·E·R OFFICES & AGENCIES

LEFT: 8881 was a half-decent D15 'Claud', one of the King's Lynn allocation and back from Stratford Works after a general overhaul. Our other D15s were 8890, 8891, 8893, 8895 with 8896 at Hunstanton until the Royal Claud 8783 arrived in early spring 1946. On the left is 'Laddy' Bridges, one of the senior passed firemen, at 45, still not a regular driver though not far off. He had a very dry sense of humour and an elder brother George, one of the three drivers at Hunstanton. Then Driver Jimmy Woods, who was a Cockney and Secretary of the Mutual Improvement Class. He also acted as Running Foreman as required and was on duty and showed me into Ted Shaw's office the day that I arrived. Like 'Laddy', he was a splendid railwayman. Next is the perennial Syd Joplin, and finally John Cook who had been a South Lynn fireman passed for driving and sadly had to come off the footplate and was transferred to King's Lynn.

ABOVE RIGHT: The South Lynn Improvement Class – part of a countrywide voluntary group run by enginemen to improve their knowledge of all aspect of locomotive design and performance, as well as rules and regulations – had an annual outing to the Science Museum in London. Apart from the acute interest in all engineering matters, the members participated in a lecture given by a senior officer in the Running Department. The author knew many of the men in the photograph who were all engine drivers or firemen at South Lynn on the M&GN section of the LNER.

RIGHT: A very quiet spell on a March Saturday when I was learning the Running Foreman's job on afternoons. "Time for a photo," said Stan Bowers, the foreman in the trilby and we went outside the little office and stores block and the two men sat on the sleepers near to the turntable. In fact, this was the makeshift buffer stop used if an engine overshot the table. There is not an engine in sight, nothing outside the 'Royal' carriage shed on the down side. Stan gave the picture its name, 'Five minutes after the bomb fell'. Syd Joplin was the 8-4 timekeeper always wearing a species of bow tie and real old-fashioned country corduroy trousers. We shared the office with the running foreman on duty. Stan was typically dressed for the part: we were not a bowler hat railway, the GE nor the M&GN come to that. Stan went out of his way to teach me everything he could about his job and the men who came his way, including March men who worked the 2150 Lynn to Temple Mills and would lodge. One or two would go round looking for trouble so they could be late at Cambridge and be relieved by a set of Cockneys going home. Stan got along well with the shedmaster, Ted Shaw, although to listen to them you would never have thought so. Likewise his opposite mate, Fred Jackson, a future Mayor of Lynn.

TOP LEFT: A Sunday morning in June 1952 in Ipswich Loco. In the background the Running Shed which held four of the 91 allocated. 1253, class B1 is standing on the short pit and has just been washed out. It will be lit up, cleaned and then work an evening job to London.

From the left: Arthur Rumbellow ('Rummy'), Running Foreman, a likeable man but a very laid back foreman; Fred Locksmith, Shed Turner, an excellent if fiery man. The turner had to be a third foreman when it came to shed arranging in that impossible shed yard. In times of stress, Fred was given to throwing his shunting pole on the ground and stamping on it. Jack Baldwin, Rummy's No. 2 was a very able man, also rather laid back, which did not always suit me. He left the railway long before his time. Harold Alen, NCT (non-clerical timekeeper) and captain of the Ipswich Loco Cricket XI for which I used to play. When Rummy was a driver, he was instructed by the foreman to take a J15 Black Goods ion with the breakdown vans through to the station where there had been a derailment in the yard. The engine was standing ready and the fireman should have checked the condition of his fire. On the way, however, the steam pressure began to fall and Rummy, with his pipe stuck upwards in his mouth, said to his fireman, "I should have a look at that fire, old mate if I was you." This he did rather unwillingly to discover a completely empty firebox. They reached the station with a struggle and got lit up with a bit of fire from another engine and some wood from somewhere. How Rummy became a foreman after that little incident remains a mystery.

TOP RIGHT: 65447 ran the Mid-Suffolk Railway whose little shed came under Ipswich where I was Shedmaster. She was always cleaned with her brasses, copper and steelwork highly polished. She is standing at Kenton down home signal at danger as it had been out of use for many months, although this was far from common knowledge. The crossing gates are across the line so the driver had stopped at the signal. In the winter of 1950–51, I caught the mid-morning train from Haughley for Laxfield. I travelled with the driver-in-charge at Laxfield, George Rouse, who spoke in the broad Yorkshire tones of Barnsley. In the late 1920s when times were hard in the north, it seemed to George that he would never be made a driver at Barnsley so he put in for driving jobs in the south and turned up at Laxfield where he and his wife and family lived happily. On the day I travelled, George drew up at Kenton home signal and sounded the whistle imperiously. The gates were across the road and clear for us but nothing happened until the porter in charge suddenly appeared and waved the train past the signal. George, however, did not move and blew the whistle again: the porter re-appeared in a fury with a green flag and waved the train forward and into the platform. I stood well back against the firebox whilst listening to the porter bawling out the driver who with nods and winks made it clear that he had the boss with him and to keep his mouth shut. The standard drill was to stop at the signal if the gates were closed (as in the picture). I decided not to re-write the MSLR personal rule book. Doctor Ian Allen who took the photo was George's family doctor!

BOTTOM: 5467, J15 and what of the train? It is a good many years since I saw a weed-killing train but here is one and the spray can be seen at work. We provided the engine for the civil engineer: plenty of branch lines in Suffolk. The driver was 'Skit' Eley from Ipswich and the train is between Wickham Market and Framlingham.

RIGHT: A dull Sunday morning in 1951 and 1535, one of the Ipswich B12s has been washed out, the fire lit and hauled out of the shed (which held four engines out of 91) to be cleaned and polished although the paintwork was unlined black and rough at that. It gives you an idea of the working conditions of those days. Soon one of the cleaners will go up a ladder to stand on the handrail leaning forward to do the top of the boiler. He stays the right side of the vertical – or else – which never happened in my experience. On the left is Tammy Gooch, Chargehand Cleaner, an ex driver who had failed as so many did with poor colour vision: he died suddenly in 1952. As he is a cleaner short of the usual four, he is doing his bit. Those 16-year-old cleaners probably started straight from school in 1950 and none of them expected to be photographed, yet look as their dress. Cleaner was a dirty job and yet all three sport a collar and tie. They will be in their mid-seventies by now. Young Rayner stands nearest to the camera but the names of the other boys has gone, nor did I see any of them grow to manhood. 1535 will go up to London with the 1800 and come back with the Norwich mail, a tough job for a B12. But her crew will make light of it: drivers Jim Calver and Charlie Parr and their firemen worshipped their old engine and her footplate was like a jeweller's shop, everything burnished. They took a pride that could never be measured in cold figures but worth so very much.

SUFFOLK L·N·E·R
IT'S QUICKER BY RAIL

LEFT: LNER poster promoting rail travel to Suffolk. Artwork by Tom Purvis.

RIGHT: Ipswich station in the 1950s, tight for room but a well-managed station where staff were efficient. Station staff with a lot to load in a two minute stop would keep one eye on their task and the other on the engine. If taking water when they were loaded, any more time over two minutes went to 'loco'. But this train is an up Yarmouth and changing engines: the fireman has unhooked and when he is back on the engine away they go to the shed. The starting signal will be replaced and the Norwich 7MT off 0952 to Ipswich will come forward and work the train to London.

LEFT: A Framlingham–Liverpool Street excursion stopping at Hacheston Halt to pick up passengers for London. The guard will get off, get the step ladder, help passengers aboard, hoist up the ladder and away they go to Wickham Market and all points south. The engine is D16/3 2552 and is worked throughout by Ipswich men.

ABOVE: 70000, Britannia, the first 7MT making its first journey to Norwich with the down Norfolkman. Driver Bill Redhead of Stratford is accompanied by Chief Inspector Len Theobald. I'm standing between the 'uprights' to wish them well on their journey.

TOP RIGHT: 'Worth Your While – Worthwhile Jobs on British Railways'. Poster produced in 1951 for BR London Midland Region to advertise employment vacancies for porters, drivers, checkers and capstanmen, detailing staff benefits and minimum rates of pay. Artwork by an unknown artist.

ABOVE: Here is 34059 'Sir Archibald Sinclair' at Parkeston Quay in 1949 when she was on trial. The Railway Executive intended to transfer what they considered to be under-used light Pacifics from West Country to the GE section based at Stratford and Norwich. Our chief, L P Parker, was a party to plans for an entirely new high-speed timetable using what he hoped would be the class 7 BR standard then on the drawing board. In no circumstances would he have any Bulleids at Stratford on a permanent basis, although the engine distinguished itself on trial with a picked crew and Chief Inspector Len Theobald in attendance. This was the penultimate day of the trials and we took a very heavy train to Parkeston with great ease in about 85 minutes. From the left: HQ Inspector Tom Sands, ex M&GN who retired as Chief Inspector, Norwich; Driver Bill Burritt of Stratford and his regular mate who later moved to Gorton; Len Theobald, an outstanding Chief Inspector for whom L P Parker had great respect.

ABOVE: Early morning rush hour at Liverpool Street station, London, 12 October 1951. This station was the busiest terminus in London at this time. During the 1940s lines into the station were electrified to provide a more efficient and faster service, although the station was still very crowded at peak times. The station is still widely used by people commuting from East Anglia into London.

RIGHT: Ipswich on Sunday morning, June 1952, north end of the running shed. 1634 'Hinchingbrooke' had just been washed out, examined with great care by Charlie Ransom, boilermaker as his chargehand Charlie Winney demanded the highest standards of workmanship. From left: Maury Smith, the giant boilerwasher; Jack Reed and Charlie Ransom, boilermakers; and a tube cleaner whose name escapes me. All four were first class men at their job. Sunday was a very busy day in Ipswich depot with so many engines requiring attention and with little or no room in which to do the necessary repairs, which were always done by the best set of artisan and shed staff.

FAR LEFT: Where else but the 'Middy'? First down train of the day over the Mid-Suffolk Light Railway leaves Haughley for Laxfield and climbs the 1 in 42 gradient, with a few passengers and some freight, Ipswich driver Ernie Baker and Ron Thompson of Laxfield. A wonderful East Anglian scene: J15 5447, the regular engine for the Mid-Suffolk by 1952.

LEFT: Old Ipswich! The 'Tram Road' with a 'Tram' in for repairs. The excellent breakdown crane, water tank and oil stores are in evidence, as is the fitting shop and the 'Wagon Wheels Shunt'. The carriage and wagon shunter is hitching a ride on the J15 5382 on her last legs. The driver is Bill Mutimer.

RIGHT: Pigg's Grave summit near Melton Constable. 2509 class D15 has brought 11 Midland bogies up 5 miles, 1 in 100. In 1950, the Clauds were well past their best which makes the work of the M&GN crew so creditable, but those men were used to small engines with heavy loads.

STEWARTS LANE DEPOT AND THE STRATFORD DISTRICT 1952–1962

05

A depot and a District, Stewarts Lane and Stratford, the former tough, humorous, and with a reputation for running trains to time, while the latter was the largest in the country. Stewarts Lane was my last shed and, in January 1955, I moved to Stratford, back on the Eastern, as Assistant to Terry Miller, the DMPS. He moved on after a few months and, early in 1959, he became CMEE of the Eastern Region and I was appointed DMPS at a time of great change, a 'Human Revolution'. This centred on the introduction of the main line diesels but there was also the November 1960 electrification of the Jazz services to Chingford and Enfield and the outer suburbans to Hertford and Bishop's Stortford. But in 1957, the then CM&EE decided that no more N7 locomotives, the life blood of the Jazz, should be given works attention nor would he see reason and we knew that punctuality of this unique service would suffer grievously. However K J Cook retired in 1958 and Mr Miller was appointed in his place, a Running man at last. Within days, he reversed the decision and a strictly controlled number of engines passed through the Works so that, in the last week of the Jazz, not one minute was lost by 'Loco', a wonderful achievement made possible by Terry Miller's decision and our dedication.

The year 1958 was very tough and one of our many problems was the extreme difficulty of finding men versed in electrical maintenance on the diesels. Before Cook retired he decreed that such work would be carried out by Stratford Works staff in normal hours and night work by Outdoor Machinery staff who knew little about locomotives of any sort. But at Stratford Running Sheds, the workshop staff had been led since the war by a remarkable man, Jim Groom, an excellent boilermaker and a welding specialist and, above all, a born leader. Since arriving at Stratford, I had started a series of informal meetings with Jim and with the shedmaster present to deal with the many matters that needed attention. No minutes, and when dealt with, a red pencil in the notebook.

But electrical maintenance was a shambles, especially at night. In May 1959 Terry Miller told me that I must take over electrical maintenance on diesels, which was great news. But with whom? Having told the shedmaster at Stratford, he asked me to see Jim who had useful ideas. Jim came up to my Liverpool Street office and asked whether I had thought of training redundant boilermakers as electricians. I hadn't, nor had I the authority to do so, but I agreed at once and so did the workshop staff at a lunchtime meeting chaired by Jim. So we started our own school. Mr Miller found us a foreman and lent us some knowledgeable men and away we went, a great success but quite without Authority's knowledge. They found out in time, raised the roof, but nothing came of it. Jim Groom squared the Craft Unions and the NUR and Terry Miller squared the Industrial Relations people at Headquarters. Job done! Years later when my old chief was dying, I went to see him. The present meant nothing to him but the past did and when I mentioned Jim Groom, his eyes lit up and we talked happily about Stratford and the Jazz until it was time to for me to go.

And now briefly the spirit of the Jazz. Driver Harry Hibbert, his fireman and I were en route Chingford with a good N7 on the 1420 from Liverpool Street. Harry had offered me the regulator and we were fast to Clapton. Running briskly into the station, I applied the brake but very little happened and we finished up at the far end of the platform. The Westo pump had stopped and refused to restart; no brake bar the age-old way with the handbrake on the engine only. We knew a Norwich fast was not far behind and the driver and I came to the same conclusion, 'on your way, pronto'. The guard was a good old railwayman and when we set off and stopped at stations, he worked his handbrake and so did we. I was DMPS at the time and asked the porter at Clapton to ring the shed at Wood Street to deal with the pump.

We arrived at Wood Street and there was Jack Barker with his tools and away we went with Jack standing on the gangway out in front working at the pump as we tackled Highams Park bank making up time. So we ran into Chingford a couple of minutes late, and in the yard Jack re-started the pump. Nothing was reported by anybody least of all me and those men would have done exactly the same had I not been there.

Here, unaltered, is part of a letter sent to me years after our retirement by Passed Fireman Reg Coote as he was in my unforgettable years at Stewarts Lane, and shows yet again the helping hand of the Brotherhood. How different is our world today!

'I started at the Lane in Feb 1941 as a cleaner, in May of that year my Mother, Sister and I were asleep in bed when we had a direct hit by a German bomb we were buried alive for 5 hours. After we where dug out by the rescue people and had a cup of tea it was 0550. I was 0600 Cleaning and in quite a state but my Mother made me go to work. On arrival the Cleaner Foreman noticed my dishevelled state I explained what had happened and was taken to the office and told that I was entitled to 2 days off for being bombed out. I asked for a note for my Mother to tell her of this she might not have believed me. Anyhow when I returned to work, two drivers came to see me, I'm sure one was Alfie Murray and they gave me about £10 which had been collected from the enginemen to give to my Mother to assist her financially after losing our home. My Mother and I never forgot this for their kindness and understanding. None of them knew me I was a new boy.'

The photograph of old 768 on page 98 shows Driver Jack May and here's 'Cooty' again: 'Jack May another great man I got on well with Jack. He was my Chairman of the SE&CR Enginemen's Sick Society when I was Secretary. I shall never know how I managed to administer the "Battersea" as the members called it. There were nearly 5,000 footplate members and I did all the admin in my off duty hours Christmas was my busiest time when I had to share the yearly surplus out to the members. They looked forward to this money as it used to pay for the Christmas turkey. Even today with old pals from the Lane or other depots they say "How much the share-out this year, Cooty." The Society helped loads of blokes financially when they were off sick I had members all over the Southern and the G.W.'

But with no typewriter or calculator nor any other modern aid, there was one way that Cooty was able to serve the men who had been so generous to a young cleaner boy and his Mother back in 1941.

RIGHT: The cab of 770 in August 1953 and the best I could do with a box camera. The low roof, round-topped firebox and high footplate combine to make the enginemen's world confined but not difficult to work in. The driver is Sammy Gingell, wearing a beret, a rarity on the SR, but Sammy liked to cut a dash in a quiet way. His mate is Les Penfold and they must have been together two years in the Ramsgate link before Les moved over to the Brick in their dual link. A typical Eastleigh footplate with Drummond fittings. The firehole door goes back to Stroudley's days on the LB&SC and to the LSWR via Drummond, his works manager. The gauge glass protectors are unique to Eastleigh with a spiked column on the right. It was said that LSW firemen kept the water level with the top of the spike. Three steam valves in the centre are for steam heat, supplementary steam for the F class exhaust injector and for the sight feed lubricator behind Les's left shoulder. High up are the steam valves for the two injectors.

FAR TOP LEFT: 123 Caley 7'0" single wheeler built by Neilson of Glasgow in 1886 to a Drummond design, preserved after its withdrawal in 1933. In September/October 1953, it came to Battersea Wharf to an exhibition of Royal stock. It was our responsibility and it was necessary to do some pretty heavy work on paint and above all steelwork. This was done by Johnny Millman, an ex fireman who was labouring in the shed yard. It went back looking a picture and Johnny did a splendid job, for his generation did nearly 30 years of cleaning and firing. From the left: Jim McTague, fitter and a Bulleid specialist, a great character from Inchicore, Dublin, with whom I kept in touch for many years; Assistant Foreman Fitter, Wal Thomas; Mr Wheeler, a visitor; me; Fred Pankhurst, Chief Running Foreman; George Kerr ('Tick-Tock', always looking at his watch), Running Foreman; Johnny Millman, Shedman; Harry Newman, acting Running Foreman; and Harry Biggs, Shed Engineman.

FAR BOTTOM LEFT: 1100 Victoria – Dover Boat Train hauled by rebuilt Bulleid Pacific. Driver Percy Tutt and his fireman John Hewing made the day memorable for W O Bentley (in the cab) and myself. W O was a dear friend. He was a Doncaster Premium Apprentice in 1906, one of Mr Ivatt's pupils in 1910 leaving the service in 1911. Before the First World War, he and his brother had the concession for the DFP motor car and during the war, he designed the rotary engines, BR1 and BR2, fitted in the first case to the Sopwith Camel fighter in 1917. In 1919, Bentley Motors was formed and the rest is motoring history. I met him in 1958 and brought him back to the railway, his first love. This was his last trip on a steam engine. We had 34101 Hartland and W O had a wonderful welcome from our crew. He sat on the fireman's seat and Percy gave me the regulator. We had a perfect journey to Dover, took the engine to the shed, prepared her and slipped across the line to the Archcliffe. We sat on our own in the back parlour and Percy and John, without realising it, got the normally reticent W O talking about his life with Bentley Motors – an hour to remember. When we got back it was my turn to do the firing. Our engine had been taken so we were given a very down-at-heel Bulleid Pacific. She was hard, hard work but we won the day and were on time at Victoria. Percy, the archetypal Cockney of happy memory, has long gone but John and I were the guests of the Bentley Museum in November 2011 and had our memories recorded for posterity.

LEFT: Artful old 'Smithy' from Deptford and his 80-year-old steam crane standing near the softener sludge tank which is an old LB&SCR Stroudley tender. Here we have the sort of men who do not normally claim the spotlight and who deserve as much of a shedmaster's time as a main line driver or Grade 1 Fitter or Boilermaker.
     From left: 'Con', whose Polish name nobody could pronounce or remember so he was Con, who worked as a shed labourer with Smithy and Frank Butowski; Tom Nightingale, Coalman, and I believe a bookie (although I did not know it at the time); Bill Price, Coalman (both men worked the mechanical coaling plant); Harry Keefe, Shed Driver; and Frank Butowski, strong and broad shouldered who liked and was worth overtime. If he didn't get it, he would swear in a comprehensive mixture of Cockney and Polish at the Chief Running Foreman who thought the world of him. He was one of the best and and if the crane 'broke down' he would make old Smithy work for a living with a shovel. Smithy was a likeable rascal who spoke very broad Cockney but in a thin, piping voice. We had to watch him but he was a real character.

TOP RIGHT: Taken in July 1957, the Sunday before Sammy Gingell's last week of service on the footplate by Dick Riley, as the three of us had a part to play in the running of that remarkable shed, Stewarts Lane, Battersea. I had come across at Sam's request for what he called 'a little sprint' to Dover on the rebuilt 34005. Sammy is on the right, a unique man who would take any engine on any train with any fireman. He had left school at 12 and had worked as a coalman's boy and then at about 14, he went off to South Wales to work down the pit as a haulier. He had his regular pony 'Cardiff' and he grew up to become the strongest of the strong with hands like boxing gloves. However, Sammy came home in 1913, got married and joined the SECR at Battersea as a cleaner aged 20. With many younger men ahead in seniority, he only had nine months in the Boat Train link but that didn't matter to him; he had done it all. On the left is the Chief Running Foreman Fred Pankhurst, who was an ex driver and had been a foreman down the Old Kent Road at Bricklayers Arms Shed. He was tough, illiterate and uncouth but he had a heart as big as a house and he saved thousands of minutes of potential lost time in finding men and engines to work the endless summer demands of the Traffic Department. He could cajole men to do the impossible, and how fortunate I was to have such support. A great shed with remarkable men who would take on anything and some of whom were 'good with a pencil' if they got the chance.

BOTTOM RIGHT: 70004 and 70014, the 'William Shakespeare' and the 'Iron Duke', are being prepared to work the Golden Arrow and, to use railway language, the second Arrow which left Victoria 30 minutes later at 1430. There is nothing unusual about the photograph, but the fact that the cleaner, who is standing on the handrail cleaning the top of the smoke box, is in a dangerous position which was an everyday risk. Nobody was ever injured!

FAR RIGHT: October 1954. We had prepared 34088 to go light to Eastleigh to return the next day from Portsmouth harbour with the Emperor of Abyssinia, Haile Selassie, who would be met by the Queen and Sir Winston Churchill, the Prime Minister, at Victoria. I rarely had my camera at work but I took photographs that day, and here are two excellent Grade 2 fitters, with both of whom I had had high words in the past for we were all three independent and strong personalities.

Hatchets were always buried quickly at the Lane and here are Syd Walker and Wilf Price, the first a Cockney from outside the gate and the second from South Wales. We had some excellent fitting and boilermaking staff and had kept them after the war when craftsmen and semi-skilled staff tended to drift away unless they were dedicated to the job, as many were, although the pay wasn't up to much without overtime and weekend work. There were plenty of jobs for the semi-skilled men on a steam locomotive, especially on the Bulleid Pacifics. The electric lighting on the Pacifics was taken care of by the electric lighting department, not our responsibility.

ABOVE: 768 about to leave the shed for the 1535 Victoria–Ramsgate, late 1954. My time at the Lane was running out and my little box camera was pressed into service for once. 768 was always highly polished and well cleaned and she looked good. Here are four interesting people. From left: Jack May, now in No. 2 link with Billy Reynolds – a splendid pair right up to the job. Jack had been the LDC Chairman and one of the best holders of the responsible position that I have ever met, straight, able, respected by all and able to see both sides of any issue. He was an NUR man elected for his ability by a largely ASLEF stronghold. He retired from the LDC in January 1954, still held in high regard, but never put himself forward again owing to the ASLEF strike in May 1955 when the NUR men ordered their men to work normally. Next, Freddy Burton, a Shed Driver with a big heart. He had been a top class fireman on the Nelsons before the war but after a while his eyes let him down and he was confined to shed limits. He was a lovely man, and so in his special way was Gerry McTague on the right, Secretary of the Workshop Committee. He was a charming and persuasive Irishman from Inchicore, Dublin, and he and Bill Brooks were a very effective pair: they did a lot for the men they represented and made sure that my life was not one of slippered ease.

LEFT: The 7MTs had been at Norwich since January 1959 when I transferred them to ease our severe shortage of staff, diesel and electric training and so on. At the end of steam in September 1962 we still had about 60 locomotives. The Human Revolution was complete.

ABOVE: A special Enfield–Hastings via Liverpool Street and New Cross Gate and Lewes, ready to leave, through 'the Pipe' (East London tunnel) under the Thames. Two J69 'Buckjumpers', 8 coaches, no condensing, made easy work for these strong little machines. Southern engine from New Cross Gate. On the left, 1500 DC electric motor coach before conversion to AC traction.

LEFT: A Stratford B1, 1280, on the 0830 Liverpool Street in September 1958 by arrangement, to give Mécanicien André Duteil of La Chapelle, Paris Nord, the experience of a Bongo on the down journey, and 70036 with Driver Ted Whitehead on the return. Andre had had the Chapelon Pacific E4 as his own and then been promoted to the De Caso Baltics, his engine being S002. He came three times to England as our guest and on the return journey in 1958, he drove 70036 from Bentley, where we were booked to stop, as far as Shenfield. He always wore his cap back to front and with his SNCF goggles resembled (as Ted said) 'The man from Mars'.

This was Ted's last week in the Norwich gang before moving up to No. 14, the L1 link, on outer suburban work. He was an outstanding driver, mate and 100 per cent for the railway. Andre never forgot Ted's kindness and his welcome – both spoke their own language yet understood each other! The 'Brotherhood of Railwaymen', of course!

RIGHT: Poster produced for BR to promote the Golden Arrow pullman day service to Paris, which operated daily from London Victoria. Artwork by an unknown artist.

ABOVE: A Ramsgate train leaving Bromley South with driver Syd Frankham. This is a 1506, class E1, on her last summer at work. She is climbing the stiff 1 in 95 incline, master of the load but hard work. The sands and steam reverser (Stirling and 1st class) are seen at work, with the driver shortening the valve travel. The coal in the tender is mixed with a lot of small stuff at the back, but her exhaust would be magnificent.

ABOVE TOP RIGHT: The final touches to 34088 before departure light to Eastleigh: prominent are the Royal buffers and the Royal drag hook and screw coupling. Next day the Royal brass beaded and polished disc boards will be set in the usual code for Royal trains. On the left is Bill Thorburn, an outstanding chargeman cleaner who worked extremely hard and led from the front. He kept his Battersea boys in order and there was never a dirty engine on his shift. Chief Inspector Danny Knight on the right was in charge of the Inspectorate at T E Chrimes' HQ (MPS) at Waterloo and rode on all Royal or Deepdene duties.

ABOVE BOTTOM RIGHT: The front of the Jubilee Shed (1897) Stratford. Allocation, in its prime, was some 555 engines. Tank roads 1–6 and tender 7–12. Tanks must have gone out for the evening peak therefore it's about 1600. Notice the shed yard is spotless. From the left: 7MT, 4MT, K3, 7MT, 7MT, 3 B1s, J19, B17.

RIGHT: Boxing Day 1954, my last week at Stewarts Lane. There are quite a few trains running including the Golden Arrow engine 34071 about to leave the shed at 1235.

LEFT: Just before the evening peak, the Enfield N7 9665 embellished by its crew leaves Liverpool Street with a one Quint. There are plenty of passengers and the fireman is well in control of the situation. He will be back again in Liverpool Street with a 10 coach load each way before the peak eases.

BELOW LEFT: Back to Stratford and a typical turntable well positioned so that an engine can be turned at the same time as it is disposed and then straight down to the coaling plant. The ever-present 'Buckjumper' is vacuum fitted with the 'Westo' brake on the engine, both used for passenger work.

BELOW: We had three little P class 'Poppers', useful and strong little engines. I loved to see one pulling a heavy load of empty milk tanks from the Milk Depot down beyond Stewarts Lane Junction: no steam at the chimney-top however cold the day and the exhaust was explosive!

ABOVE LEFT: The working of the Jazz out of Liverpool Street to Enfield Town and Chingford in the peak hours was one of the wonders of the railway world. I have a photograph of Signalman B Alsford in vigorous action in Liverpool Street West Box and below, thanks to David Butcher, the railwayman and author, is a resumé of Alsford's duties during the evening peak in July 1946. 'In his box, the signalman would continuously be operating the signals, points and block signalling instruments seeking clearance over the down suburban for each departing train and then "Train entering section". Alongside this he will be receiving and sending similar bell codes for trains coming to him on the up line. On average, every 10 minutes, he worked something like 26 point lever movements, controlling some 40 individual sets of points, about 30 signal lever movements controlling 30 signals and 24 sent and received bell codes – some 80 actions or one every 7–8 seconds, in addition to which he had to keep a sharp lookout for anything untoward outside his box. He would maintain this work rate for some three hours with little

respite. The trains to and from platforms 1–4, used but one pair of tracks, the up and down suburban which ran the full length of Bishopsgate Goods so that every 10-minute cycle meant four trains over the up line and another four on the down, all with manual signalling. The Jazz was unique: occasionally I would look down from the West Side bridge and watch every move, great railway-work.'

ABOVE RIGHT: The famous Pilots at Liverpool Street. 9614, west side: 8619, east side. All brightwork was scoured and polished daily. Levelling pipes above the tank burnished for the first time by George Chittenden. Both engines stood ready to cover failures, 9614 first choice, 8619 station shunter.

RIGHT: Liverpool Street Eastside platforms 11–18. From left: N7 with empty stock for Thornton Fields; B17 1647 on Ipswich line train; a Cambridge B1 1283 en route to the turntable and what looks like a standard 4MT. The train on the extreme right is a Southend 1956 stock.

LEFT: The photographer is standing above the Main Stores and the Water Tank and looks down on a disposal pit where the Digger is loading ashes into wagons headed by a Buckjumper. On the right is the 'New Shed', actually built in 1871, which is used purely for the maintenance of engines. There is no ventilation so all engines in the shed are 'dead'. Three of the six roads in the shed can be seen; No. 1 for diesel shunter maintenance, 2 and 3 for X day examination rigorously on a time and mileage basis. Nos 4, 5 and 6 are out of sight, 4 and 5 being devoted to boilerwork and 6 to special examinations to engines with defects difficult to detect (plenty on steam locomotives) and preparation for special duties. In short, 6 road had a very experienced staff who took on whatever came their way.

A variety of shunting engines are standing in front of the shed, which would be hard at work on a weekday, and maintenance is always done on a Sunday. To the left with light-coloured doors is the Paint Shop, part of the Works, but Mr Gabbitas, the foreman, was a good friend of ours. The blue East Side Pilot at Liverpool Street was thus painted in 1958 with the authentic GER blue, stored away these last 40 years. All the rest, except the buildings behind and beside the railway are Works property, No. 2 Carriage Shop on the left but our Crane Shop is partially hidden by steam. Beyond and opposite to the foot-crossing are the MIC classrooms containing many sectioned locomotive components for the instruction of up and coming enginemen.

The Crane Shop foreman is the legendary Breakdown Foreman Syd Casselton. He was brilliant in his use of the 36-ton crane and of the German re-railing equipment. His priority was to clear the main line as quickly as possible and, once started, Syd would brook no interference of any sort that would delay the resumption of traffic. Several of his prized breakdown men worked in the Crane Shop as fitter's mates and would stop what they were doing to get the crane and vans on their way within 30 minutes, usually less. Others lived outside the gates and when called out were on the job in minutes.

RIGHT: Poster produced in the 1950s for BR to promote the company's rail services. The style of the artwork makes a marked break from the typical poster art of the period, which was generally rather conservative. Artwork by B Myers.

BELOW LEFT: Stock poster produced for the SR showing the Bulleid Pacific locomotive travelling at speed along the tracks. Artwork is by Leslie Carr, who painted marine subjects and architectural and river scenes. He designed posters for SR, LNER and BR.

BELOW RIGHT: July 1953; a demonstration of the German Railing Equipment of which Stratford was the first depot to be so equipped. Bill Hunting, the breakdown foreman is at centre, while on the left is Sir Michael Barrington-Ward of the Railway Executive, a formidable figure who struck fear into many but never in the bowled-hatted figure on the right, the great L P Parker, Motive Power Superintendent Eastern Region. By the time I came back to Stratford in 1955, L P Parker had retired and died the following year, deeply mourned by hundreds of men who came to his funeral.

RIGHT: The back end from the Coaling Plant facing east. The J69 is shunting a raft of three tank engines to release 7720. The J20 is fresh from general repair as is the B1. With endless marshalling and an enormous shed, foremen, shed turners, and artisan staff have a job on.

SOUTHERN RAILWAY

FAR LEFT: From left: Running Foreman Bill Tindall, Chief Running Foreman Arthur Davey, and myself, Assistant DMPS Stratford. We are standing in front of 90602 at the new (1871) shed, probably in 1957. The 350HP shunters and eventually the rest of the Stratford shunting fleet were maintained down Nos 1 and sometimes 2 roads and the maintenance was of a high standard, because Ernie Button, the chargehand fitter had been dealing with these engines since 1944. What he and Les Thorn, who eventually became my diesel assistant in 1959, didn't know about those little machines would go on the back of a postage stamp. Arthur was one of the most energetic and dedicated of men, given to chewing pencils and humming to himself. He was scrupulously fair and he was never defeated by the endless problems of running a shift in the steam days at Stratford.

LEFT: Bishopsgate platform (station closed 1916): B17 1600 on up Yarmouth service. On the left are the up and down suburban lines in the tunnel. Above is Bishopsgate Goods depot and to the right is Shoreditch (Metropolitan) for the East London line.

ABOVE: Artwork showing advertising hoardings at a London station, *c.* 1962. Railway stations were a good place to advertise, as they would be seen by large numbers of people as they waited for their trains.

ABOVE: 70039 is very much a Stratford engine coming up No. 10 at Liverpool Street at 1355 on the dot. She will stop under the hotel, quiet and smokeless. 70040 is in No. 9 with the 1424 Norwich via Cambridge. 70039 had three great drivers, Bill Shelley, Geo Warren and Ernie South.

RIGHT: Fred Smith (fourth on the left and clearly in charge) and his oil squad. Fred was the chargehand selected to organise the special arrangements at Stratford to counteract hot axle boxes and bearings on 350 steam locomotives. This was one of L P Parker's specialities and the arrangements were very satisfactory in reducing the number of over-heating bearings.

06 SNCF EXPERIENCE
ON NORD AND EST REGIONS
1958 – 1971

An invitation to travel on the famous Chapelon Pacifics from Calais to Paris could not be declined and it opened the door to the SNCF and its staff. How those French railwaymen loved visiting us and realised that we were not the unfriendly and reserved 'English' after all!

This is part of an article written in 1986 for a rather special book on France, it's hotels and restaurants by Richard Binns and its title was *French Leave Favourites*. He asked me to compare the life of a SNCF steam driver and one recently charged with the working of the TGV service from Paris to Lyon. This is the first half with some additions and minor changes which describes a journey that I made on one of the great De Caso Baltics, the 232S003. The mécanicien was André Duteil and his magnificent chauffeur, René De Jonghe. The text is non-technical but one must say that the S003 was in its last weeks of service and that André's own S002 was already laid aside. These engines were stoker-fired and therefore the fire had to be maybe 6in thick over the grate and the feed to the grate constant and directed to perfection. The coal was the size of small pebbles, perfect for stoker-firing and to get the hottest steam possible, the water was carried in the bottom nut of the gauge-glass throughout the journey with the utmost confidence. The temperature in the superheater was between 400° and 420° Centigrade which is very hot indeed.

'It is a warm summer evening in 1961 at Aulnoye in Northern France. Steam traction has nearly done on this section but tonight André, René and I are going to draw wonderful work from our old locomotive, the S3, which has but a month to go before being laid aside for ever. André, the mécanicien, is 5ft tall, a little gold-toothed, pink faced ball of fire of 48 who knew all about the Railway Resistance during the war, a marvellous driver, artistic in his use of the brake: René is one of the best of firemen, tall, strong, quiet and immensely experienced. L'Equipe Duteil/De Jonghe come from the historic depot of La Chapelle, under the shadow of Montmartre. I know the road so André motions me to take charge of the locomotive. It is hot in the cab but when we are moving the wind will freshen us up although the fire will become blindingly white, requiring constant attention over the enormous grate; our faces will soon be black with coal dust and certainly the bucket of water hanging outside in the cool air containing bottles of citron will be needed for we shall have to think and work hard tonight.

We are away with a huge packed train of 780 tonnes and the S3 soon gets into her stride. One does not need to press her with that load, but nevertheless, because we are late and time must be regained, we are going to reach our maximum permitted speed of 120kph quickly and then hold it, uphill and down-dale. This will need constant and careful adjustment of the controls and speed of firing, an intimate knowledge of the route, gradients and the position of the signals, for in the left-hand corner of the cab, under my only lookout window, lies the speed recorder which tells me everything I want to know but also charts the speed – *L' Espion*, the spy! And how different from this country where one rarely if ever encountered a speedometer until near to the end of steam.

'And now the light has gone, a wall of blackness lies ahead of the long boiler for no headlights probe the darkness: stations flash by, Le Cateau, Busigny, one's head outside in the wind to pick up, as soon as they appear, the green signals that beckon us on, our old engine tearing into it, René in his element, for we are living parts of our machine which depends on the courage and skill of its crew. We are in a world of our own, cut off from authority, from our passengers, from every living soul except those in distant places who control the signals.

'We stop only once, at St Quentin, running up the long platform as fast as possible to save a few seconds, for every little counts. On again into the night, Tergnier, Noyon, Compiegne and then, as we approach the great junction near Creil, first yellow, then red lights bar the way but the road clears as we pass slowly through the station. We have lost some of the time we regained from Aulnoye, so now the S3 is opened out to shoulder her load, thundering up the long rise, spitting sparks of defiance high into the sky. On through Chantilly, over the viaducts, she gradually accelerates to 100kph, before we reach the summit near Survilliers, passing under 'Le Pont de Soupirs', momentarily illuminated by the open fire-hole door. And now our work is done, I hand over to André and we can spin silently, but ever vigilantly, down to Paris.

'As we climbed through Chantilly, Andre had served a good Bordeaux, brought specially for the occasion. Having uncorked, tasted and approved the wine, very much at room temperature, we drank to the great days of steam and to our own good fortune. At length, we drew quietly to a stand in the Gare du Nord. We have covered 134 miles in 132 minutes and, as we look down at the passing throng, we knew that we had reached the end of an era.'

André and I had become firm friends after my first journey with him in April 1958 and since then he had visited the UK five times, sometimes to stay in London with James Colyer-Fergusson and to meet our railwaymen and travel on our engines. So many things were different: loose coupled freight trains were almost unheard of in France, engines without speedometers *encroyable* but the warmth of his reception was always unforgettable. I can see him now at Dover Marine running down the Invicta's gangway in his blue overalls, cap, scarf and goggles ahead of the passengers and then his typical Cockney reception on the Bulleid Pacific from Harry Wing and Peter Warner of the Lane.

RIGHT: What a picture of strength and control: March 1960 just before electrification to Amiens. Len Theobald, our Chief Locomotive Engine Inspector, who loved France and got on very well with the railwaymen, travelled back with me from Paris on Train 19 with the Calais men on E46. It was a wonderful journey and the engine was never worked hard despite a very heavy train. The mécanicien was Henri Odent who was nearly 50 and on the verge of retirement, and his enormous chauffeur, Robert Gourdin, in his later forties, seen here smoking a Gauloise, in far from vigorous action as he flicks the coal in the firebox with what appears to be a spoon in his formidable grasp. Apart from the back corners of the grate, the shovel hardly went near the door. The E46 looked a picture as can be seen overleaf, a credit to the work of both men as was the economy of coal. Incidentally the large brickettes can be seen stacked in the tender. Normally they are only used to build or rebuild the fire and a hammer blow breaks them in half as required. Excellent fuel when used for this purpose and roused up by the long poker when leaving a terminus.

LEFT: This is a wonderful Gallic silhouette: precision, concentration, left hand on straight air brake to get the exact speed of 15kph on the recorder for an emergency track repair. Remember that *L' espion* will have a record of his speed and that 9.2mph is very slow on a locomotive to be maintained over a distance with a heavy train on level track. The Conducteur is Amadee Gosnet from La Chapelle, one time Senateur Paris/Orléans who had been getting the very best out of his magnificent 16000BB, an electric locomotive which had to be driven! – nothing boring about handling these machines. At first our driver did not quite know what to make of his English guests when we joined him at Amiens. But by the time we had reached Lille we were in perfect accord.

ABOVE: The Gare du Nord, Paris, March 1959: 231 E46,one of the last Chapelon Pacifics to be built in 1936/7 for the Nord, working the Flèche d'Or, train 19 to Calais. E46 was the *machine titulaire* of mécanicien Henri Odent and his chauffeur Robert Gourdin who were complete masters of the job. On the left is Philippe Leroy, the head of the Motive Power Deptartment on the Nord Region of the SNCF, a very dear friend, and when he retired in 1970, all his BR friends had him and Madame over to see them off in our warmest style. Alongside him is another old friend, Len Theobald, Chief Locomotive Engine Inspector under L P Parker.

ABOVE: It's 1960. While we were taking water, M. Maire of La Villette (the Stratford of Paris) discovered that the left big-end was running warm and the Chief Inspector M. Gabrion, who was riding with us (an Est Region regulation), is assisting him in dealing with the situation. Incidentally, the engine came off the train as booked at Bar-le-Duc and we took it back to Paris without further incident. The engine was a 241P, basically a PLM design modernised by André Chapelon, the only time that I have even seen one of the breed, and I was not particularly impressed.

ABOVE RIGHT: François Joly had the K73 from Amiens to Calais. We have just left Boulogne Tintelleries climbing up towards Wimereux, 1965. François has his hand on the wheel that controls the amount of high-pressure steam passing to the low-pressure cylinders. Below are the reversing gear and the small wheel which controls the degree of variation of the blast pipe orifice.

ABOVE: An early journey in 1961 with Henri Dutertre (right) and his BR cap but with his new fireman, Arnaud Flament (left), who was champion billiard player of the SNCF Nord as well as becoming, after a couple of years with Henri, a firing instructor – in French *moniteur de chauffe*. Here he is with his bright eyes, and his tendency was at times to disagree with Henri. James Colyer-Ferguson, who died in January 2004, took me to France in 1958 and we returned many times. Henri was the first French engineman that we travelled with in April 1958, which was a remarkable experience, it also amazed the Frenchman that I was capable of firing the Chapelon Pacific, which I did from Amiens to Paris. It was the first of many weekends spent with James or the other BR railwaymen who came with me. We gave Henri a BR cap but the only way you could wear goggles that were provided on the SNCF was by reversing the cap so that the peak was at the back, much easier with the normal blue soft cap of the SNCF men.

ABOVE: A classic, which includes me, René de Jong, André Duteil, George Mitchell and M. Jean Kerleau, the Ingenieur en Chef at Aulnoye in 1961. I had been driving, and from the chimney of a stoker-fired engine comes a solid stream of fine gritty coal, so goggles were essential, as was a good wash but we had no time for that until we got to Calais via Lille! René was a magnificent fireman not far off retirement and he kept an unvarying boiler pressure and water level from start to finish and anticipated every move necessary to achieve the perfect journey. George Mitchell was the Examining Inspector for the Eastern Region passing men for driving duties.

RIGHT: A happy photograph at Amiens in 1965. George Barlow (see overleaf) is on the right along with M. Andre Corbier, the Chief Controller in the Amiens 'Permanance' (the Control at Amiens). George loved coming to France and that morning, with Train 16, he had had hold of the E9 for several sections and acquitted himself very well. The train was very heavy and it was necessary to have two engines, which was nonsense for the E9 could have handled 700 tons on her own without trouble, but towards the end the engines were treated gently!
     From left: Henri Dutertre with his E9; Michel Rock, his fireman; the inimitable Raymond Lasquellac, 'Dunstable', who had a cousin living in Dunstable; and his mate Fernand Chaussoy, an élève mécanicien. This was the first time that I had met Raymond and his hilarious attempts to pronounce Dunstable (Doonstarb), St Albans (Sant Olbons) and Whipsnade (Vipsnard) were highly memorable. The man standing in the middle with scarf and hat is the Amiens Train Dispatching Foreman.

BELOW: This is Jacques Vidal the first time I travelled with him in 1961. We are not far off Vesoul, our speed drifting down and now was the time to take some pictures. We are going at 116kph on the *L' espion* and Jacques is a happy man for I had done the firing and much to his approval. There is no room in front of the driver for *L' espion* so it has to go over the other side and the mecru has to glance across to see that the speed is within the limit of 120kph on this stretch, although the Es, K, and Gs can run at 130kph, track permitting. As I write both Jacques and Jeannine Vidal are in their nineties and these last few years my two sons and I have regularly visited their home near Troyes. Each time Jacques has written and always says that the champagne will be on the table ready to drink at 11 o'clock sharp!

RIGHT: George Barlow's favourite photograph, taken in 1967, of the SNCF visitors who he called 'The Old Firm', a title unknown today but often used for a group of soldiers, sailors or airmen who had served together and who were great comrades. George and Maurice Vasseur were two men completely at one with the other yet neither could not speak a word of the other's language. But what an example this is of 'The Great Brotherhood of Railwaymen', the true membership of which transcends all boundaries of rank and position. Maurice was a Chapelon Pacific mécanicien with 231E7, a Calais engine whose chauffeur was Louis Sauvage. Louis had been a Boulogne fisherman who had joined the railway in his twenties and had been firing for many years on the fast trains between Calais and Paris. George was the engine driver in charge of the Romney, Hythe and Dymchurch Railway

and had his own engine, the 'Green Goddess', built in 1925, and he arranged a ride for his visitors. He had tried to join the LNER at Colwick, Nottingham in 1934 as an engine cleaner en route to firing and driving but there had been no vacancies. He joined up early in the war and became a sergeant instructor for Royal Engineers potential drivers and firemen. Demobbed in 1946, he joined the Romney, Hythe and Dymchurch with whom he gradually became a legendary figure known all over the world.

BELOW: Henri Dutertre and his last mate before the diesels came, p'tit Louis Lapierre (little Louis) who had fired for years on the E17 on the Paris jobs, a gentle giant whose shovel looked like a pencil in his enormous hands. They are running into Calais Ville with train 19 with the job well done (largely by me)and it is a splendid study of a happy Equipe. Their engine was 231G81 and they shared her with René Gauchet, both he and Henri top class men. As I write, Henri, a year older than me, is in pretty good form but his gigantic mate only lived a few years after retirement at 50. I met him once and he certainly wasn't the man he had been. But as a general rule, drivers and firemen on the SNCF retired at 50 and could not they believe that ours used to be perfectly happy to carry on to 65 – indeed there were very sound reasons why they should do so if their health stood up. By contrast the French locomen started a new life and Henri, for example, has had all but 40 years of retirement. As I write I've had almost 30 years in retirement and I still love to go to railway gatherings to enjoy the of men I worked with or heard of many years ago.

OPPOSITE: 12 March 1966. Train 27 loaded to close on 650 tons has arrived at Boulogne Ville with a 141R of the later series with Box-pox coupled wheels and the Kylchap exhaust. These were thrilling, powerful machines, American design modified and greatly improved by Chapelon and used all over France. When this photo was taken, Henri Dutertre was sharing 231 G42 with René Gauchet, who has the engine that day. Henri has worked the 0800 Calais Ville to Amiens returning with train 27 after which the Calais boys took us out to dinner. On this occasion I had taken my dear friend Colin Morris who was still at King's Cross as Divisional Running and Maintenance Engineer. Despite his frequently sombre appearance, Colin was perhaps the most amusing man that I have ever worked with and also a very fine engineer and railwayman who was grossly underestimated by his seniors in the GN line days. He and I had a perfect relationship both on the job and off it.

ABOVE LEFT: After arrival at Jeumont, our activities had included servicing the engine, walking heavy laden to the Jeumont messroom, a distinguished lunch with various wines, a walk across the Sambre Canal to an auberge for cognac and coffee and finally here we are resting as we wait for our train to arrive from Belguim. From left: Henri Douillet, the senior chauffeur at la Chapelle and normally titulaire on the U1, André Duteil, me and the author James Colyer-Ferguson. We were, of course, in prime form despite our lethargic appearance. (See also overleaf.)

ABOVE: This is a lovely study of Edmond Godry and myself in 1969 outside the dormitory at Calais. Steam had not yet gone but the Pacifics had left Calais and the 66000 BB diesels were doing the job after a fashion but with no regularity. On this journey I had John Shone, a close friend from my Liverpool days, with me, and we had 141Rs to Boulogne, back to Calais, then passenger to Hazebrouck in an Autorail and back to Calais with Edmond as our guide. Our drivers were 'Dunstable' (Raymond Lasquellac), Roger Chabe, Champion Boule Player SNCF Nord who had been in charge of the 231K22, and Claud Scrieve who came on the scene too late to be a Pacific Mécanicien, a 'Senateur'.

ABOVE LEFT: In the messroom at Jeumont, 1962. We have had a marvellous lunch and will soon be ready for off after we have been across the Sambre for cognac and coffee. We have already prepared our engine for the return journey to Paris.

ABOVE: Harry Noden, Carriage and Wagon (C&W) Assistant Liverpool Street, and Arnaud Flament are enjoying themselves on the E9 between Amiens and Calais, Henri Dutertre, the driver, out of sight. On the left are (top) the control wheel for the ACFI feedwater heater (a delicate touch is required). Below that is the lubricator for the pump and the handle protruding gives you a visual idea of how fast the pump is working. The wheel below is the water control for the right-hand live steam injector. Harry was a mechanical engineer who specialised in carriage and wagon maintenance and design. He came to work with us when the C&W department was merged with the Motive Power department as well as the Road Motor and Outdoor Machinery departments.

RIGHT: I was invited to represent BR on the last steam-hauled train from Paris Nord to Calais in May 1971. At Amiens, and having finished an excellent lunch en route, I was hailed by M. Ravenet, the CME of the Nord and ordered to travel on the engine to Boulogne wearing my best suit. Getting up onto the K82, I found that M. Leseigneur, the retired and legendary Chief Inspector of the Nord was already there and in post-prandial form. He was immediately followed by Oscar Pardo and so we were six. But about two minutes before departure, a steward arrived and passed up three splendid steaks with all the trimmings and two bottles of vin rouge, side plate and glasses and a delicious pudding to follow. So the principal contestants were 'out of action', huddled in the fireman's corner enjoying their meal whilst the regulator was appropriated by M. Leseigneur which left me to do the firing in my best suit.

07

TRAFFIC AND DIVISIONAL MANAGEMENT

1963—1973

By the end of 1962, departments had merged and I realised that I could tackle General Management. I was appointed Divisional Manager first to King's Cross and then to Liverpool. At both places we had a grand management team and we really did make things hum. Open meetings with the staff gave us great satisfaction.

After several months acting as locomotive engineer for the Eastern Region, it was decided that I might be capable of becoming a divisional manager but that I must have some experience before a decision could be made. So, in November 1963 I became the acting Traffic Manager at Lincoln, not without some qualms as I was new to Commercial matters and limited on Operating matters, although it was in my blood, whereas on the Running and Maintenance side, my main aim was to give Ken Taylor, the District Motive Power Superintendent, as much of a free hand and as much help as I had been given at Liverpool Street by Harold Few.

And so it was that I found myself going to a distant meeting on a bitterly cold and windy evening, barely a fortnight after my arrival at Lincoln. My colleague, Derek Burton, was a very able railway officer but he would possibly admit that, in 1963, he was no expert at the mundane task of keeping his diary straight and his secretary had great difficulty in getting her chief to come to the point. It so happened that myself, Derek, and a young man called Frank Patterson who was on the threshold of a splendid career were on our way to Spalding by car to meet the Coal Trade (to me, a terrifying ordeal) on the contentious subject of coal concentration, whereby the railway delivered coal to a central point and the coal merchants had to come and get it, whereas in the past, they were delighted to use a full wagon of coal as a bunker on wheels on their local goods yard instead of it being used for another journey: Doc Beeching was dead right on this one as in so many others. On the way, Derek reminded me that he was meeting the Coal Traders of Boston the following week but somehow (and beyond his comprehension!) he was also billed to debate the closure of the railways of East Lincolnshire with a NUR Organiser, in public, at the roaring metropolis of Barton-on-Humber.

Derek had great charm, especially on such an occasion, and I found myself agreeing to stand in for him at Barton-on Humber without the slightest practical knowledge of the subject and over the coming weekend I tried to brief myself, although the more I learned, the less I seemed to know. On the day, Bill Boothright, our railway chauffeur, drove me through rain and sleet to arrive at Barton in what seemed to be total darkness. My spirit had sunk to an all-time low but my imagination was at full throttle for I could 'see' the hall, packed to bursting point with livid Bartonians, baying for the blood of the 'cretin' who was proposing to close their railway. I could 'hear' the jeers of derision and cat-calls as I made my faltering case whilst round after round of applause would no doubt greet the skilled invective of the NUR orator. I longed for the assurance of a Beeching, the charisma of a Fiennes, and the profound experience of a Johnson and, just now, I had none of these things. But I had asked Albert Bostock, the Grimsby sales assistant, to come along as part of the audience to bail me out and for this and many other things, I owe him a debt of gratitude.

However, it was 1800 when I arrived at the home of the gentleman who was going to chair the meeting. The welcome I received steadied my nerves and during dinner, my railway life came up for examination. When I mentioned the Southern and its amazing Bulleid Pacifics, a certain look, well known to me, came into my host's eyes and I knew that I was on a winner: a bargain was struck and in return for a nice little sprint to Bournemouth and back, he would see that I had a reasonable ride later on in the evening. Wine, good food and delightful company began to work its magic and when we arrived at the hall, I felt that I could take on the world. The world, however, proved to be not 300 infuriated Bartonians but some 20 pleasant and enthusiastic folk, most of whom were railwaymen of whom three were from the Guards LDC at Grimsby. The NUR organiser was a Docks man and the last thing he wanted was a public debate on a subject of which he knew about as much as I did. So we each said our piece and sat informally on the table answering questions, assisted, nobly, by Albert Bostock. It was a thoroughly enjoyable railway gathering in which the minute audience participated civilly and effectively and said they were glad to meet me! My baptism of fire was over and never again, however severe the opposition, was I to feel so lost and forlorn, although I had still to learn many lessons on the importance of preparation and the dangers of extemporising in public. And as a matter of interest, Barton-on-Humber still has its railway!

The life of a divisional manager was endlessly interesting, enjoyable, difficult and challenging. Above all, in my sort of division, I dealt with people, the most fascinating study of all. My last division was Liverpool, where I dare to say that I was well known and respected by our huge staff and I had a first-class management team who were truly worthy of the name. But although we did a first rate job and achieved many economies, I was not a 'bottom line' man and therefore seen by the new top brass as no longer worthy of promotion in General Management with a big reorganisation pending that was to eliminate the divisions so let us confine ourselves to people in these few words in the King's Cross and Liverpool Divisions.

At King's Cross, Reg Clay, a wise and experienced staff assistant who had started on the GC in 1917 as a boy messenger put it to me that we ought to re-start the informal communication meetings with our staff so that they should know what lay ahead that would affect their lives: these meetings had foundered during my predecessor's time. We did start to the tune of three meetings covering the division every six months and, knowing how my predecessor had fared, I dreaded the first meeting for the audience would contain the sardonic and able Charlie Evans, Goods Checker, and the explosive Bert Goldfinch, who represented the cartage staff at the Goods, not to mention the smiling, conversational and very shrewd Steve Watts as was that legendary veteran of many a Top Shed battle, Driver Bob Lunniss. In fact the meeting of over a hundred men was tough, hard hitting and humorous, yet correct. One was given an extra strength to handle the meeting and wonderful support from my management support. We kept this going and the reaction when I told the staff at a much later King's Cross meeting

TOP LEFT: Burgh-le-Marsh on the East Lincs below Willoughby, 1964. Bert Webster and Harry Amos admire the work of the proud station Foreman. Bert had been my assistant and true colleague when I had been at Liverpool Street. When he joined me, I was 35 and he was 57 and we balanced each other perfectly. He had retired when he visited us at Lincoln and greatly enjoyed his day out with Harry and myself judging stations and seeing a part of the railway unknown to him.

TOP RIGHT: These were some of my right-hand men during my short stay of 7 months at Lincoln preparing the district to enter (against its wishes) the new Doncaster Division in June 1964. From left: Ernest Needham, Chief Clerk, Harry Amos, District Operating Superintendent, and Jack Luty, District Traffic Inspector. There was a degree of comfort in the old coach and it served us well; always know as the 'Special'.

BOTTOM LEFT: The 'Special'. AGN body and frames on Gresley bogies? Anyhow, the old coach rode very well and enabled me to see much of the district in a short time. Bill Boothright, my chauffeur, looked after the cooking for lunch and opined that he would like a footplate trip. So, on one of the journeys with an elderly B1, I put him aboard and told the driver to get cracking! Poor Bill, who had been a BR motor-driver and had also been through Dunkirk in 1940, was scared out of his wits as the old Bongo knocked up a healthy 70mph. 'Never again, I'll stick to the road in future!'

BOTTOM RIGHT: Preparation for an Eastern Region Board visit is bad enough but when they are accompanied by two ferocious BRB members, Philip Shirley and Fred Margetts, men wanted to put up the shutters. So one goes over the route beforehand. We are at Collingham and the Board arrived from High Marnham (where I joined them) and we came in to Lincoln via Skellingthorpe and Pyewipe. The Central Station Master, Mr Chadwick, and I successfully weathered a Shirley inquisition. Then to St Marks via the East Yard where Shirley pinioned me in a corner with the unanswerable question: "Why have you got two stations at Lincoln, Hardy? Get one closed at once." We passed the carefully screened 1874 Midland Pullman doing duty as a messroom and we set off for Collingham where I left them to it. Our little team had done a good job and the visit was a success. Our engine is a B1 1406 with our inspection coach and, from left: Station Master Collingham, Jack Luty, Harry Amos, Derek Burton, Norman Micklethwaite, Sheila Hazard, my secretary, Ernest Needham, Bill Boothright, with three enginemen behind and a goods guard.

TOP: The Castle class 7029 had just arrived at Peterborough for a month's work in the hands of New England men who did very well and enjoyed themselves. The years is 1967 and John Betjeman looks down in the classic pose of the old GWR drivers and behind him stand Reggie Hanks and, beyond, Horace Botterill, Foreman Fitter of vast GN and LNER experience. He and his staff worked hard on 7029 which pleased Pat Whitehouse, the owner and, in conversation with W O Bentley, with whom he had much in common, they agreed that they had seen worse jobs than a Swindon engine but 7029 could not really stand comparison with the products of Doncaster. Reggie Hanks preserved a masterly and amused silence.

BOTTOM LEFT: In March 1968 Burton men were working a train of fly ash from Drakelow Power Station to the Fletton Brick Pits. The driver did not know the road beyond Stamford and picked up a conductor at Toton. After the usual crawl through Peterborough, they took the Goods Line which permitted trains, in clear weather, to run at very reduced speed and be prepared to stop clear of the train ahead. As they moved up slowly, Aubrey Dolman, who was the Burton driver's mate, shouted that there was a red light ahead, but the driver took no notice and, seconds later, they ran into another fly-ash train: both drivers were killed instantly and Aubrey was trapped and unable to move.

The breakdown cranes from New England and Finsbury Park were in position and the rescue men hard at it by the time I arrived to join Colin Morris. The problem was the impossibility of using burning tackle to free Aubrey, and a heavy wagon was entangled with what was left of the cab, a menace to the life of the trapped man. By 0400 two alternatives were left: the amputation of a limb and the end of a driver's career as an engineman, or a grave risk to be taken involving the use of two cranes to make a lift of a few inches under great stress. All I had to do was to take a decision without hesitation. This risk was taken with delicacy and precision, a way was created, and Aubrey was borne away to hospital. He had smoked his pipe and talked to his rescuers, and had the courtesy to thank us all.

BOTTOM RIGHT: The group shows us from left: Colin Morris, Divisional Running and Maintenance Engineer, King's Cross; John Betjeman; Edwin Howell, Divisional Movements Manager; the great W O Bentley and myself at Wansford, which was then in my King's Cross Division. The photo was taken by Reggie Hanks, ex GWR pupil, trained at Swindon under C B Collett. From Wansford to New England, we propelled our old GN saloon (lovingly restored and now on the Bluebell Railway) and our three guests occupied the armchairs at the front of the coach whilst we watched where we were going over their heads.

that I had attending a meeting with the BRB which proposed the closure of King's Cross station and concentration on St Pancras. At my last meeting before I left for Liverpool, I was able to tell the gathering that the plans had proved unworkable – to prolonged cheering!

And so to Liverpool, a new world far away from the Euston HQ, which was respected when that masterly GM, Bobbie Lawrence was in charge. He let us get on with the job but he had us all nicely taped. So I started the same but renamed review meetings, which were most successful and enjoyed by many of those who came, for one of the great advantages was that people met each other informally before and after a meeting who would otherwise never have crossed paths. But there were moments: at my first meeting with the staff of the Area Managers Birkenhead, Northwich and Ellesmere Port, relief signalman Raymond Dickey of Hooton rose both to his feet and to the occasion. Never had I had such a lambasting as the blood rose up his neck and he became scarlet with indignation as he informed me that he had no love for divisional managers and little respect for them. I kept my temper and, in time, gained his respect and when I left in September 1973, he bought me a little gift that I shall always treasure. I loved those meetings in the Liverpool Division and they served their basic purpose of drawing management and staff closer together. And they were usually humorous! Except for one at Garston. A certain very senior BR officer was visiting the Division to 'meet the chaps', so we called a day-and-a-half of meetings in which he insisted on being Chairman. I introduced him at every meeting and then, rightly, took a back seat. Question-and-answer was going well when a Garston driver who had asked the first question (he usually did) and been well satisfied with the reply, rose to raise some other issue. The Chairman was going strong with the reply when the questioner thought he had got it wrong and interrupted him, whereupon the Chairman shouted at him: "Will you bloody well shut up and listen". That was the end of the meeting: the audience broke up and walked out; they simply would not have that sort of behaviour from the railway's top man. It was second nature to me to deal with such an interruption and, "Just hang on a minute and let me finish", would have had that audience of hard-bitten railwaymen in the palm of his hand.

ABOVE: Euston about 1987. In the centre is Jack Cherry, a much-loved GP in Abingdon who was going with me to Liverpool for the first time and also to watch Liverpool play at Anfield – a rugger man through and through! For a short time, the London jobs were manned because of the mileage limitation by two drivers out of the top link, and here are Arthur Owen and Tommy Perkins, both Scouse comedians, to entertain Jack and to educate him in railwaywork for both were able men. On arrival and after introductions, Jack climbed into the cab to be greeted with, "Now you're here, Dochter Sherr-ie, wah about a free consultation?" What a happy journey it was too and the return journey was the day of the Bushey disaster so Jack saw railway work in the raw on the way home.

ABOVE: I was Divisional Manager Liverpool from May 1968 to September 1973, the experience of a lifetime. We took our Saloon, which we shared with the District Engineer, out on working inspections, which were hard but necessary and enjoyable. This is August 1973, my last outing before leaving the Division and we are at Delamere CLC when the station had a signalbox and a species of yard. From left (standing): Arthur Williams, my deputy and a truly good one; the incomparable Danny Whelan, Operating Superintendent; Arthur Behrend, who lived near our Wirral village of Burton; Ken Lord, Maintenance Engineer, who had been reared on the Southport electrics and later on the MS&W section; Roland Lancaster, the first commuter to rumble me (the service was so bad from Chester to Rock Ferry that I did not disclose my hand at once); Denis O'Reilly, Area Manager, Northwich, once S M Mullingar, very Irish and a really good railwayman; Jack Appleby, pillar of the Mail Room and excellent relief Steward; Peter Summers of JS&S, now part of BSC, dedicated to steel-making and a good friend; Jack Berry, our Guard and Inspector for the day and Fred Lancaster, a farmer and brother of Roland. From left (front): Alan Newitt, at Edge Hill in the 'Extra' link; John Connolly, our much-loved Steward; George Bordessa, Driver, once of Edge Hill and presently at Garston depot; and finally the remarkable Reg Holmes, Delamere Signalman and character.

ABOVE LEFT AND RIGHT: On 11 August 1968 a special train was run from Liverpool Lime Street to Carlisle via Manchester to celebrate the end of steam traction on British Railways. I travelled on the Black 5 45110 to Manchester, and the photograph shows the Deputy Mayor of Liverpool and his daughter in the driving seat, and Driver John Hart, a 1924 man who must have done over 20 years' firing and completed 46 years' service. Brian Bradley, his fireman, would have been passed for driving shortly afterwards. The Chief Inspector of the LM Region, John Hughes, was in overall charge and he was amazed at my request (as a newly appointed Divisional Manager) to put a few rounds on the fire during the journey. In the evening I went to Lime Street to welcome the train home and here I am with Fred Smith, also a 1924 man, and his fireman Steve Roberts. Like the morning men, they came from what was left of Edge Hill depot, a shed with a great reputation for fast running and variety of work. I was just beginning my time at Liverpool and I knew even then that I was going to enjoy the Scousers, although whether they would admire me was another matter!

ABOVE: For the time that Driver Fred Griffin had her along with Charlie Rolstone and Charlie Sampher, 70037 'Hereward the Wake' was kept as in the photograph, a joy to behold. Much work was done by the enginemen themselves, as well as the cleaners, and like all our 7MTs she was a splendid engine at her work. Until the maintenance of our Britannias began to fall away in 1958 – a very hard year for us all – they were as good as the Norwich engines, although not a soul at Norwich would have agreed! 70037 is standing at Cambridge waiting to return to London with a special train and 'Griff' and his mate have been hard at work: the cab would be sparkling and all steel, brass and copperwork re-polished yet again. Fred wears his uniform cap with the GER Bat's Wing above the peak, overall clean on every day, highly polished boots, but there was nothing fancy about him; he simply loved and had pride in his work. He knew, too, that his time would eventually be up in the Norwich link and then he became an early diesel instructor. He also brought the first 1250hp Brush diesel into Stratford Works in October 1957. His son Laurence was a driver for Enfield in charge, along with two other sets of men, of the beautifully kept N7 9665. Regular manning was the main reason that in the last week before electrification in November 1960, not a minutes was booked against any engine working the Jazz services from Liverpool Street to Enfield and Chingford. Steam really did go out in a blaze of glory on the Jazz, where, in the peak, there was a steam-hauled train climbing Bethnal Green bank every two-and-a-half minutes.

ABOVE: Car being loaded onto a British Railways Eastern Region train. This train transported both passengers and their cars, allowing people to go on holiday by train but still take their cars. This service began in 1955 between King's Cross and Perth and proved to be successful.

ABOVE: Signalmen at work in the interior of the Willesden Signal Box, North London, during the British Transport Films production *Willesden Signal Box* made in April 1966. How things have changed.

From the Centre Georges Pompidou · CCI · Paris

"ALL STATIONS"
A JOURNEY THROUGH 150 YEARS

An exhibition at the Science Museum
22nd May – 27th September
Nearest Underground: South Kensington

ABOVE LEFT: Exhibition poster produced in the 1970s for the Science Museum, London, to advertise their exhibition on loan from the Centre Georges Pompidou in Paris, France – a fantasy portrayal of railway station and trains.

ABOVE: Every day that she worked the Golden Arrow, 70004 had to match the beautifully appointed Pullman coaches, not to mention the onboard staff and conductor. She was cleaned by the senior cleaners on duty, and one of the five did nothing else but brightwork, steel, copper and brass, of which there was a great deal. You will notice the inch-wide band round the buffers, which was achieved with emery cloth, but copper and brass was done with what we called 'Derby paste'. She was an excellent engine slightly less powerful than her sister 70014, but the cleaners who stayed with the railway will always remember cleaning this beautiful machine. Following wet weather she would come home plastered in mud and at 0600 next morning the cleaners would start all over again. Many, many years ago, before the First World War, almost every engine was kept like that: look at them in the York Museum and you will see 737, class D of the SECR. She was a 'Coppertop', and she is in the glory of a livery that could never be contemplated today, but when she was new, she also worked the boat trains to Dover.

RIGHT: Northwich was in the Liverpool Division in Cheshire. The picture shows a Stanier 8F working a freight train in the Chester direction. The train is between Northwich and Hartford and Greenbank on the Cheshire Lines, and I have a passing interest, because before we left Liverpool I purchased a station lamp which contained a paraffin container and lamp from Greenbank station. Wherever she is going, the track will not be level on the CLC, which includes a climb to Cuddington and the Delamere Forest.

THE YEARS BEFORE AND AFTER RETIREMENT

1973

ONWARDS.

08

By 1973, I was nearly 50, DMs were to disappear and I came up to the BRB at Marylebone to a job that I grew to love, a job in the making and the perfect job from which to retire at the peak. So, with that very useful financial inducement, I retired at 59 and life has been truly full and happy.

In October 1973, Gwenda and I left Liverpool and our home in the Wirral with a heavy heart. I knew that my career was at the crossroads and that I should not realise my ambitions in General Management. It hurt at the time but I knew in my heart that it was the right decision. Initially I was responsible for the career development of all professional engineers in the Mechanical and Electrical and the Signal and Telecommunication as well as in the main workshops (BREL) from their recruitment up to a level where their careers could be encompassed by the BR Management Development organisation. But I had the priceless advantage right from the start that I reported to the Chief Engineers and not to the Director of Personnel. When I left Liverpool, there were 5,690 people in my Division whereas in my new job, I had a lady clerk, Mavis, and Janet, my secretary, skilled in shorthand, and we worked hard and moved mountains in the end. Mavis retired just before me, Janet got married and was replaced by Margaret, and what a happy little team we were. I was involved, if I so wished, in every engineering appointment up to a certain level and I am glad to say that my previous career had prepared me well for what my job eventually became.

As my responsibilities widened so did my influence but only because I managed to overcome the stranglehold of red tape by cutting it but never forgetting to tie it up again after the job was done. Up to 1975, the proud and independent Department of the Chief Civil Engineer wanted no truck with me but then, the defences were lowered and I began to get to know as many of the younger men in training and well into their careers as possible. I loved working with the Civils and their Regional Chiefs were glad to take advantage of my experience. I had worked closely with Civil Engineers especially at District and Divisional Level..

By and by, I became involved with the top management grades and then finally with senior officers. By this my own staff had been increased by another clerk, Linzi, to help Mavis, but by about 1979 I was advising the Director of Engineering as well as the chief engineers on appointments and they generally took my advice which did me a power of good. Of course the divisional managers, most of whom I knew so well, had engineering managers, most of whom were on my lists and what a joy it was to rescue an able man from a dead end or working for the wrong man and then manoeuvre him into the right position working under the right man. I remember my Director disagreeing with my recommendation of an engineer to fill a very senior post. I told him his choice was the wrong one and he took my advice after I had stuck to my guns and appointed the hardened fighter that was the right choice under the circumstances.

Not always as rewarding as that but in the main, a marvellous job with a great deal of influence and, above all, a sense of humour was vital and also a certain strength of purpose. I had made a recommendation to a certain divisional manager and he appointed someone else by no means suitable. I knew the reasons and it was no surprise to me to hear "that he had told Dick Hardy to get stuffed". Two years later, I found myself in a similar situation and I took a chance and strongly recommended a good man but by no means the right one. My old colleague fell for it and appointed the right man for the job whom I wanted but had not recommended. A chance but it came off and both of us were happy for different reasons and the old boy never knew he had been conned!

The photograph on page 152 shows Alf Murray clipping the ticket of a lady passenger. Alf had been a driver at the Lane, the first man to whom I spoke to ask the way to the office of the DMPS who was going to brief me about my new job. He was a remarkable and a truly good man who had started at Battersea in 1917 and, in my time, was in No. 5 link, the Chatham goods link that had a great deal of passenger work in the summer. When he retired from the footplate, he started a second career at Ashtead where he lived as a railman with responsibility for the car parks and many other duties. All the passengers liked and respected him and his knowledge of the railway, train times and what was likely to happen when things went wrong. He knew most of the drivers on the electrics as after steam was finished at the Lane, he had transferred first to become a motorman at Leatherhead and then to Dorking North. So he knew the form and stayed in that job until he retired a second time when he was 80. He was a real railwayman, an engineman, a good ASLEF man and he appreciated a management that got things done. He lived until he was 94 and I went to his funeral as did many other men from the Lane, one of whom was Percy Abeydeera. This is a letter that he left for me when I left the Lane which I treasure.

> Dear Sir
> It is with regret that I learned that you were leaving us so soon. Without any fear of contradiction I can honestly say that Stewarts Lane has benefitted by your short period of Shedmaster.
> An official who can demonstrate with his own hands how a job should be done gains the respect if not admiration of all thinking footplate men.
> For what you have done and tried to do at our Depot during your stay the majority of us I am sure are grateful.
>
> Yours respectfully
> Driver A Murray

RIGHT: Appleby and most of Julian Riddick's normal team back in the early 1980s. His A4 4498 named 'Sir Nigel Gresley' is in the yard at Appleby having worked from Carlisle and would work forward to Hellifield where the train reversed and was worked round to Carnforth, Lancaster and Preston. A perfect trip, although Julian was at the throttle part of the way and he was a rough handful when he was performing. The A4 crowd were first class as were the greater part of those in charge of the various steam locomotives in those days. Some such as Tom Tighe, a real Yorkshireman, are still hard at it and here you have the 'Gresley' and they were a pleasure to work with. From left: Robert Riddick, Terry Wheland, Julian Riddick, John Graham, Norman Hugill, George Gordon, Chief Loco Inspector at Carlisle on his last steam trip before he retired, Eddie Gibbons, Ian Howson (head next to nameboard) BR driver, firing for the day, Davie Hine, Driver, the PW ganger at Appleby, Ben Hervey-Bathurst, and my guest with me about to work my passage. Julian was a dear force to be reckoned with: it was he as much as anybody who put me up for election as Chairman of SLOA (Steam Locomotive Operators Association), a task that I greatly enjoyed and who would ring me up at 11 o'clock at night and sound off about some supposed injustice and try to enlist my support. He usually had his way, but if not, he would tell me that I was "a bloody bureaucrat", and a few minutes later, "Well, goodnight ,old chap, you always do your best for us." I had the honour of speaking at his funeral.

LEFT: Here we have Don Dutton, Jack Beaman, John Robinson ('Robbo') and myself together with the LNER K4 3442 'The Great Marquess' in apple green livery, based in 1999 on the Severn Valley Railway, in perfect condition in every department. To have a day with these three splendid railwaymen was an annual event. From left: Don Dutton, a volunteer who spent many happy hours on the footplate as John Robinson's fireman as well as days in the workshop; then Jack Beaman, still on BR as a Saltley driver and the Chief Loco Inspector of the SVR. I am between jack and John; John was the mechanical foreman at Bridgnorth and had a driving turn from time to time. I was very much at home on this LNER engine, except that 3442 lifted her safety valves for she would steam on a candle. In March 2010, back on the SVR, she was a very different engine and never got near to lifting them. I realise now that the Scottish fireman who was present seemed rather keen for me to have a go, which of course I did but with minimal success: later we found out how much dirt there was on the firebars.

ABOVE: The 'Rocket' with Bold Cooling Towers in the background in 1980. From left: Jimmy Donnelly, then the senior passed fireman at Edge Hill, Captain Bill Smith, the owner of the old GNER 1247, J52; Peter Hardy, out for the day; Fred Dale ('The Principle Boy'); and Wilf Hulme, next in seniority to Fred.

ABOVE: In the cab of a diesel shunter whilst enjoying a naming ceremony, hosted by Southern General Manager Gordon Pettit at Stewarts Lane. One of the many photographs taken in April 1988.

LEFT: Liverpool Street station was built in two parts. The first part was built between 1871 and 1875 by the Great Eastern railway to serve the east of England, to the designs of the engineer Edward Wilson. It was a 10-platform station set below street level and had a very unusual cantilever truss roof. In 1892–4 another eight platforms were added with a roof of similar design. The Great Eastern Hotel was built in 1880 and in recent years has been completely refurbished and is now a five star hotel.

LEFT: Clipping a lady's ticket at the barrier is Alf Murray. When the photograph was taken he was a day or two short of his 80th birthday and he lived until he was 94. Bombed out twice during the war, he was evacuated to Leatherhead where I was born. He was a splendid driver and much liked by everybody, helped his comrades whenever he could, and as far as I was concerned, it was a joy to work with him. He had started in 1917 and become a fireman in the Nelsons before the war: his Nelson had the Lemaitre blast-pipe fitted and Alf always said she was a flyer. He did great work as a passed fireman getting driving turns during the war and especially in the air raids. When I was Divisional Manager at King's Cross, I sometimes travelled to Surbiton with him and enjoyed driving and above all stopping with the old Queen Mary stock. When he reached 65, he had already been an electric train driver some years based at Dorking and as he lived in Ashtead, he applied for a railman's position at the station. He became the passenger's friend, looked after the car park, helped people who were in difficulties over travel arrangements. He loved his work for he was well known by all the Western Section motormen some of which had started at Stewarts Lane and had even fired for him.

RIGHT: Annually, the Cambridge University Railway Club was given an E4-2785 – the last to survive. BR provided two coaches, a driver, a fireman, and inspector to give the young people instruction in driving and firing. Here she is entering Bartlow with an undergraduate at the regulator (if not the brake). A great event.

LEFT: Here is my friend 'Blanche' (along with the 'Linda') at Boston Lodge and against her stand a good cross section of the Locomotive Department, both permanent staff and volunteers. I had 10 years on the Ffestinog Railway Company Board from 1977–87, an unforgettable and bracing experience and by no means an easy ride. So here we go

From left: Clive Gibbard, a member of the permanent staff of great experience as a craftsman and engineman; Colin Dukes, who served the railway as locomotive engineer for many years; Paul Ingham, with whom I pared up for four days each year as his fireman and we really had a splendid time together. Oil-burner firing fascinated me having had experience many years before of the old Austerity 3152 at March in 1947. Then Alwyn Jones, a volunteer of many years standing, as was Jo Clulow behind him and whose father was one of the Company's doctors. Jo gave a great deal of time to the railway, not only on the engines but on the Operating side and in the Control. Then John Davis and Colin Sudland who were both volunteers at Boston Lodge; the little chap next to him is 'Shadwell', who was a Welshman with very Welsh names, which defeated many of the English staff – Llyn Aploto, so he was known instead as 'Shadwell'. These days I understand he runs his own engineering business and that there is a copy of this picture in his office. And if I have got the spelling wrong, will somebody please correct me! Then comes Roy Harper, a volunteer at the Lodge and finally Andrew Arrowsmith who was known as 'Arry which went well with his surname.

RIGHT: Between Sunday, 31 March and 6 April 1985, the replica Gooch 8Ft Broad Gauge Single Wheeler paraded on a straight stretch of track in Hyde Park opposite the Albert Hall and she was named the 'Iron Duke' by the Duke of Wellington on 3 April. I was co-opted by Major Olver of the Railway Inspectorate to pass out drivers from the Kent and East Sussex Railway and I recruited Bert Hooker ex Nine Elms to train the drivers while I passed them out: not a difficult task as some of them were BR drivers we knew well. What a sensation that huge engine with its enormous chimney must have created in 1851 when she could spin along with a light load at 70mph but she had no brake on the engine, only on the tender. (How did you stop in those days? You reversed the engine and gave her steam, an unofficial practice that survived to the end.) Putting things into perspective, the boiler came off a WD Austerity tank engine, as did cylinders and crank axle, Stephenson valve gear reversed became Gooch fixed link gear and the carrying wheels came from an 08 diesel shunter but you would never have known it. From left: Mike Hart, Managing Director of Resco who built her; Tony Hall-Patch stands on the step wearing his old Royal Engineers cap; then Bert Hooker and John Higgins who, along with John Sinclair and others, actually built the engine. The 'Iron Duke' was a wonderful machine and above all, I had the pleasure of meeting Tony Hall-Patch. He and his staff did a remarkable job, the detail of which is set out in an article 'The Iron Duke re-born' written by Tony in his capacity as Assistant Keeper in charge of Transport at the Science Museum.

LEFT: When I retired in 1982, a number of kind people who were not necessarily BR but other railways and folk who had a love of the railway, railway work and our job decided to give me a present to mark my retirement. In fact I had been able to give them permission to travel on the footplate, visit signal boxes at busy times and so on. James Colyer-Fergusson organised the evening and Basil de Longh had a wonderful whisky decanter cut by an excellent firm in North Walsham. It is a much treasured gift.

RIGHT: There are not many pictures of this device for raising steam on overloaded or shy-steaming engines. This is a 'Jimmy', otherwise known as a razor or, on the GE section at Ipswich, as a 'Spike'. It was an illegal but vital piece of equipment if the 'Little Black Goods' were to be constantly overloaded and run to time. Its purpose was to increase the sharpness of the exhaust which in turn produced a marvellous white-hot fire and a firework display at the chimney top, as well as a constant supply of steam at maximum pressure. And all for half a crown paid out of the back of the hand and in this case, to the blacksmith at March Loco in 1913 by Fireman John Lilley of Parkeston who gave it to me at an ASLEF Dinner at Parkeston in 1960. This work of art was made out of the company's material and in the company's time and fixed across the blast pipe whereupon the two lugs fitting inside were locked into place by the thumbscrew with the safety chain as a backup. Its so-called razor sharp V-section bar across the blast pipe did the trick by increasing the smokebox vacuum thereby drawing the steam producing fire ever whiter. It made those old J15s steam very freely. When John Lilley, deep in retirement gave me the Jimmy, he also gave me a blow-by-blow account as to how it helped him to maintain steam with a 'Little Black Goods' on 45 of bacon from Parkeston to Spitalfields. This took nearly as long as the journey and was John's swansong for I never saw him again.

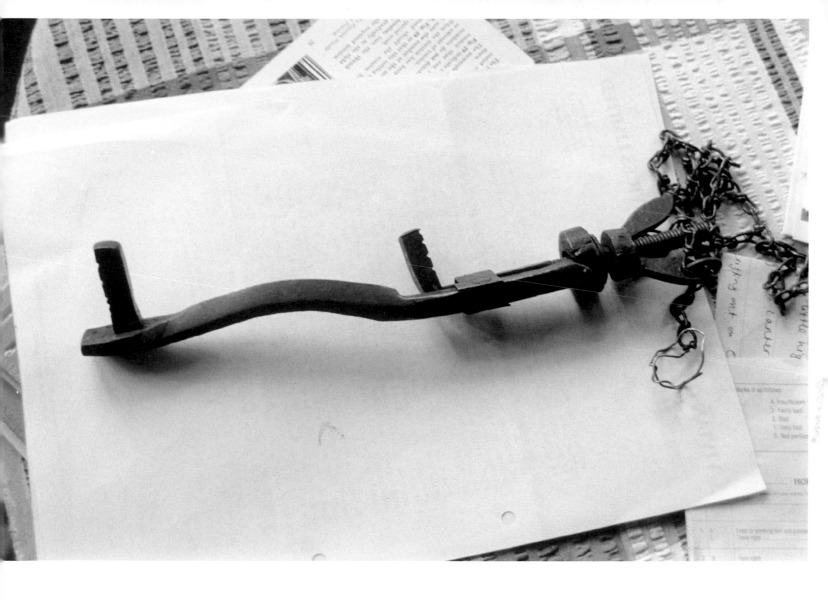

RIGHT: 27 July 1986 between Warwick and Banbury, driver Vic Waites and 'The Old Stoker' then a mere 63-year-old flicking the coal into the back right-hand corner of the grate. It was very important to keep the back corners replenished. There is plenty of heat in this fire and I'm wearing a glove to protect myself. Tea cans are on the tray. Vic has the regulator well open and is driving with a short cut-off, and economically. This is what this old engine likes — 4498 class A4 'Sir Nigel Gresley', one of the best.

ABOVE LEFT AND RIGHT: Much of this book is about personalities and I am thankful that my career included working with so many railwaymen, literally thousands of them. One still sees them as if they were alive and as full of character as ever, and for that reason I am putting them at the end of the book long after our time together, for I feel that they will bring back the atmosphere of those days long past. The photographs were taken in 1963 by Driver Jack Searle and he gave me about 20 pictures of different men, mostly taken after I left the District. Here are Albert Page and Ted Whitehead, both 7MT men, Albert on 70001 and Ted on 70036, both engines well cleaned and all copper, brass and steelwork beautifully burnished, their nominated engine in which they took great pride.

GLOSSARY

ADMPS Assistant District Motive Power Superintendent

ASLEF Associated Society of Locomotive, Engineers and Firemen

Bongo The early B1s on the LNER had the names of Antilopes. 8306, a Stratford engine was called Bongo and the Cockneys used it as a comical nickname which was universal at Stratford.

Bulleids O V S Bulleid was Chief Mechanical Engineer of the Southern Railway: his Pacifics were known as 'Bulleids'.

Carr Loco Doncaster Running Sheds which were nearly a mile south of the station.

C&W Carriage and Wagon

CLC Cheshire Lines Committee

CME Chief Mechanical Engineer

CM&EE Chief Mechanical and Electrical Engineer

DMPS District Motive Power Superintendent

Doncaster Plant Works included carriage building and repairs

Duration 'We will do this for the Duration', i.e. to the end of the war.

GC Caprotti Italian Caprotti valve gear fitted to four class B3 Great Central Railway locomotives

GC Great Central

GER Great Eastern Railway

GN Great Northern

Gradients Indicated by gradient posts. The steepest incline on British railway system is probably The Lickey incline which is just south of Birmingham at 1 in 37.

GWR Great Western Railway

IR Industrial Relations

K&WV Keithley and Worth Valley Railway

Lanky Slang term for men who worked on the Lancashire and Yorkshire Railway

LB&SCR London, Brighton and South Coast Railway

LDC Local Departmental Committee

Link Top Link is usually 1, fast main line expresses etc. Usually the summit of an engineman's life. Goods link is usually lower down say 5–8. Promotion is by seniority.

LMS London Midland and Scottish Railway

LNER London and North Eastern Railway

Loco short for Locomotive Running shed

LSWR London & South Western Railway

M&SW Midland and South Western

Mecru Short for mécanicien de route

Met & GC Metropolitan and Great Central Railway

MSLR Mid Suffolk Light Railway

NER North Eastern Railway

PWG Permanent Way Ganger

PLM Paris Lyons and Mediterranean Railway prior to 1938

SECR South Eastern and Chatham Railway

SNCF Société Nationale des chemins de Fer Français

Southend Code After 1948, all steam locomotives were fitted with a coded shed plate Southend 30D

SR Southern Railway

Stewart's Lane Battersea Large Running Shed covering work on the Eastern and Central Sections of the Southern Region.

Stirling, Pat Patrick Stirling was the Locomotive Engineer of the GNR from 1867–95.

Surtees boiler Robert Surtees was Chief Draughtsman of the SECR 1899–1913. His boilers were very free steaming and easy on maintenance.

SVR Severn Valley Railway

Woolwinder was a Gresley Pacific 2554 and named after the St Leger winner of 1907. All bar two of the A1 and A3 class were named after winners of great races. The horse was actually named Wool-Winder